More Than Pizza

Youth Ministry Beyond Our Culture and Ethnicity

By

Tony Gryskiewicz

All Scripture quotations, unless otherwise indicated, are taken from the Holy Bible, New International Version®, NIV®. Copyright ©1973, 1978, 1984, 2011 by Biblica, Inc.™ Used by permission of Zondervan. All rights reserved worldwide. www.zondervan.com The "NIV" and "New International Version" are trademarks registered in the United States Patent and Trademark Office by Biblica, Inc.™

Scripture quotations marked (NLT) are taken from the Holy Bible, New Living Translation, copyright ©1996, 2004, 2015 by Tyndale House Foundation. Used by permission of Tyndale House Publishers, Inc., Carol Stream, Illinois 60188. All rights reserved.

Material from *One Body, One Spirit* by George Yancey. Copyright (c) 2003 by George A. Yancey. Used by permission of InterVarsity Press, P.O. Box 1400, Downers Grove, IL 60515, USA. www.ivpress.com.

Material from "A Cross National Analysis of Church Based Youth Ministries." by Len Kageler used by permission from the author 22 January 2018.

ISBN: 978-0-9998711-0-2

Table of Contents

Acknowledgments

To my beloved wife, Anna; my best friend, and my greatest encourager.

"The man who finds a wife finds a treasure, and he receives favor from the LORD" Proverbs 18:22 (NLT).

Preface

Shortly after arriving at our family's new assignment at Vienna Christian Center (VCC) in Vienna, Austria, we found ourselves planning a "youth unity night" for the various youth groups that comprised the youth ministry at VCC. While we had ministered cross-culturally for decades in the United States and Europe, never had we ministered in such a culturally diverse atmosphere. Over eighty cultures call VCC their church and this cultural diversity is reflected in the youth ministry. So, it was with a little trepidation that I approached this first meeting with the youth leaders to plan "unity night." Among one of the first topics of discussion was what food should be served after the youth service. Without hesitation, someone suggested pizza, and the other leaders quickly agreed. As I processed this, my mind began to spin with new questions and ideas. Pizza seemed to be something all the youth groups (and the youth) had in common. Were there other things that they had in common in relation to youth ministry? Would Josh McDowell's "6 A's" of Youth Ministry from *The Disconnected Generation* be relevant in a multicultural context?[1] If so, what would they look like? Would the principles from Doug Fields's *Your First Two Years in Youth Ministry* be applicable? More importantly—more than pizza—what else did these multicultural teens have in common? What are the characteristics of healthy multicultural youth ministry? This document, the result of a three-year quest, attempts to answer that question.

---

[1] The Six A's of youth ministry are Affirmation, Acceptance, Appreciation, Affection, Availability, and Accountability. For more information, see Josh McDowell, *The Disconnected Generation: Saving Our Youth from Self-Destruction* (Nashville: Thomas Nelson, 2000).

Chapter 1

The Harvest

Imagine an orchard with many different types of trees. Everywhere you look there are different kinds of fruit trees growing next to each other. Apple trees growing next to peach trees and pears are growing among orange and cherry trees.

You have been commissioned by the owner of the grove to harvest the fruits, but you notice many of the workers who are partial to apples are only harvesting apples. Others, who prefer oranges, are harvesting only oranges and still others are only harvesting plums or pears because those appear to be their chosen fruit. These workers often ignore the low-hanging, easy-to-reach fruits of the other trees to focus on their selected fruit. A few even pluck their chosen fruit out of other harvesters' baskets (but that is another topic for another day). The thing that strikes you the most is that the harvest is not all being brought in because some trees are being neglected or ignored due to the various preferences of the harvesters.

This illustrates the status of many (if not most) of the churches and youth groups in the United States and Europe. Have you ever noticed that most churches and youth groups are usually ethnically and culturally homogeneous? As we will see later on in this book, most churches are not multicultural or multiethnic. Could it be that, like the harvesters in our illustration, we are focusing our efforts on our "chosen fruit" even though there are low-hanging fruits of different types all around us?

As pastors, youth pastors and youth leaders, we have a tremendous opportunity to reach young people from every culture and ethnicity with the gospel of Jesus Christ. The time (and the fruit) is ripe; we just have to be willing to reach *all* cultures and ethnicities with the gospel. Now, like never before, a prudent youth worker can reach teens of many different cultures and ethnicities for Christ.

This book has been designed to help you ask some challenging questions about your ministry and to help you develop core competencies in reaching and ministering to multicultural and multiethnic teenagers. Think of it as adding another tool in your youth ministry toolbox that will better equip you to carry the gospel to teenagers regardless of their cultural or ethnic background.

As Christians, we believe that the gospel is for everyone. We believe that Christ's atoning death on the cross is available for whoever will call upon the name of the Lord. For the most part, however, we tend to hang around people that look like us and talk like us… and we tend to evangelize among people who look like us and talk like us. Yet, the gospel is for everyone! I am convinced that there is an incredible opportunity before the church; an opportunity to get out of our Jerusalem and Judea and to take the gospel to our Samaria. An opportunity to cross ethnic, cultural, and societal boundaries to reach people who don't look like us or perhaps talk like us, with the gospel; to reach our Samaria if you will allow me to phrase it so. As I will point out in this book, the time is right and young people are ready to engage in cross-ethnic and cross-cultural relationships like never before. A youth ministry that is intentional to understand the characteristics of healthy multicultural youth ministry and that is intentional to reach their Samaria will not only be fulfilling Jesus's mandate in Acts 1:8, but will also experience a harvest of souls for the kingdom of God.

2

While many books have been produced on the topics of cross-cultural youth ministry and multicultural churches, little has been written specifically about youth ministry in a multicultural context. However, there is a vast library of materials written about multicultural and multiethnic churches, as well as work by cultural anthropologists and the insights of missiologists on ministering to different cultures. In a practical ministry sense, missionaries have been working cross-culturally for centuries, but local pastors and youth pastors tend to be monocultural in focus. As youth cultures shifted and the church maintained its ministry model, many churches were unprepared for the mass exodus of youth leaving the church.[1] By sifting through the materials in cross-cultural ministry as well as missiology, it should be possible to glean insights into principles and characteristics applicable to youth ministry. This book, which is based in part on thirty years of qualitative experiential analysis in youth ministry, is an attempt to identify key characteristics that are present in healthy multicultural youth ministry.

Vienna Christian Center is a thirty-year-old international church in Vienna, Austria. The population of Vienna is approximately 1.8 million. Of this number, nearly 1.1 million are from other countries. In other words, over 60 percent of the population of Vienna is foreign born.[2] Other than at churches like VCC, in a city where over half of the population is from another country, why should people care about multicultural youth ministry? Isn't most of the world homogenous when it comes to culture? Aren't most churches, especially in the United States,

---

[1] Terry D. Linhart and David Livermore, *Global Youth Ministry: Reaching Adolescents around the World (Ys Academic)* (New York, NY: Zondervan/Youth Specialties, 2011), under "Youth Ministry Changes More Than You Know," Kindle.

[2] Vienna City Administration, *Vienna in Figures 2015* (Vienna: Vienna City Administration, 2015).

culturally and ethnically monotone? What does the Bible say, if anything, about multicultural churches? As ministers to youth, it is important to remember that society is not culturally neutral nor do teenagers encounter God in a cultural vacuum.[3] Culture plays an important role in how teenagers perceive God and how they come to know God.

---

[3] Benny C. Aker and Gary B. McGee, eds., *Signs and Wonders in Ministry Today* (Springfield, MO: Gospel Publishing House, 1996), 64.

Chapter 2

---◦◦---

Key Concepts and Questions

Before delving too far into these and other questions, it is important to define some key terms that are pertinent to the discussion of culture, ethnicity, and multicultural ministry.

Culture

The late Paul Hiebert, a missiological anthropologist and professor of Missions and Anthropology at Trinity Evangelical Divinity School, defined culture as "the integrated systems of learned patterns of behavior, ideas and products characteristic of a society."[1] Culture, like language, is socially transmitted. In other words, culture is conveyed by the older members of society to the younger members. Often, this is done non-formally, but it can be accomplished formally and informally as well.[2] The way people dress or where they sit at the dinner table or what festivals they celebrate, as well as the foods they eat (or do not eat), are products of culture.

---

[1] Paul G. Hiebert, *Cultural Anthropology*, 2nd ed. (New York: Baker Academic, 1997), 25.

[2] Aker and McGee, *Signs and Wonders*, 65.

Culture, according to Dr. James Plueddemann, is comprised of three parts. These include worldview, practices, and values. Worldview is internal; that is to say, it deals with the "philosophical assumptions about the purpose of life and the nature of reality."[3] A person's worldview provides a structure by which that person categorizes his or her perceptions of reality.[4] Practices, on the other hand, are the visible, external things that people often notice about a culture, such as language, music, and food. Linking worldview and practices together are the cultures values. These cultural values are "ideas that link abstract philosophy (worldview) to concrete practices."[5]

Researchers like Geert Hofstede and Robert J. House have done extraordinary work in the field of Cultural Anthropology, having attempted to measure, analyze, and quantify culture. House and the team working with him published the book, *Culture, Leadership, and Organizations: The Globe Study of 62 Societies*. Among their findings, they were able to group similar cultures into what they called *clusters*. The researchers then placed similar cultures together and dissimilar cultures further apart. Observing Country Clusters according to Globe, one would see that Anglo culture (i.e. USA, Canada, England) is most similar to the Germanic and Nordic cultures and most dissimilar to Middle Eastern cultures.

Hofstede is probably most famous for developing his cultural dimensions theory, which he published in his book, *Culture's Consequences: International Differences in Work-Related Values*, in 1980. The cultural

---

[3] James E. Plueddemann, Leading across Cultures: Effective Ministry and Mission in the Global Church (Downers Grove, IL: IVP Academic, 2009), 71.

[4] Charles H. Kraft, Christianity with Power: Your Worldview and Your Experience of the Supernatural, Reprint ed. (Eugene, OR: Wipf & Stock Pub., 2005), 195.

[5] Plueddemann, Leading across Cultures, 71.

dimensions theory posits that every culture can be rated on six cultural dimensions; Power Distance, Individualism, Masculinity, Uncertainty Avoidance, Long Term Orientation, and Indulgence.

In Figure 1: The United States in Comparison with Austria and the Philippines, three countries are compared using Hofstede's six dimensions. In the Individualism dimension, it is observed that the United States has a high score of 91 (the highest in the world, followed by Australia and the United Kingdom) while Austria (not to be confused with Australia) scored 55 and the Philippines 32. The Filipino score of 32 shows that they are a collectivistic society that cares more about the good of the group than the good of the individual. Cooperation, in Filipino culture, is emphasized more than competition. In the United States, however, competition is stressed over cooperation, and so are individual achievement and "standing on your own two feet." This chart illustrates how two cultures might clash. American and Filipino teenagers working and serving together may quickly find their cultures conflicting as the Filipino perceives the American as selfish and not supporting the group, and the American perceives the Filipino as passive and lacking initiative. The greater the difference between these dimensions, the greater the potential for cultural misunderstandings and tensions to arise.

Figure 2: Potential Frustration Level illustrates the significant gap between American and Filipino culture and the great potential for misunderstanding and frustration when these two cultures work alongside each other. Ultimately, when it comes to culture, there is no "right or wrong; rather, different cultures represent different creative approaches to life--each with areas of strength and areas of weakness."[6]

---

[6] Kraft, Christianity with Power, 182.

Figure 1: The United States in Comparison with Austria and the Philippines.

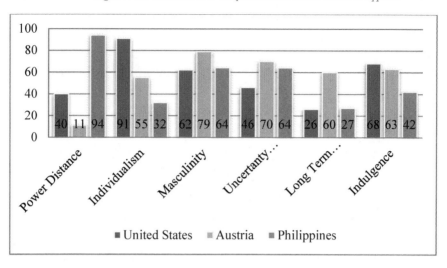

Source: Geert Hofstede, "Country Comparison," The Hofstede Center.

Figure 2: Potential Frustration Level

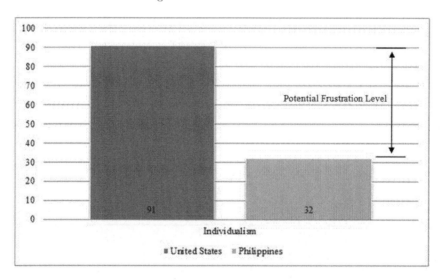

Ethnicity

The *Merriam-Webster Online Dictionary* defines *ethnic* as "of or relating to large groups of people classed according to common racial, national, tribal, religious, linguistic, or cultural origin or background."[7] In its most basic form, ethnicity is a set of biological traits passed on to someone by parents and ancestors.[8] Since the late seventeenth century during the era of exploration, when many countries in Europe began to colonize other continents, a common ideology emerged that attempted to classify the different groups of people encountered.[9] It was not long until most of the intellectual elite were referring to the three races: Negroid, Mongoloid, and Caucasoid. George Yancey writes that "ethnicity refers to groups that have cultural distinctions while race is used to denote groups that are perceived to be physically different from each other."[10] However, there is only one *race*, the *human race*. While it is given that there are variations in skin tone, eye coloring, and other physical features, human beings sharing traits from one ethnic group are capable of breeding and producing viable offspring with members of other groups sharing different ethnic biological traits.

The term *race* has often been used interchangeably with *ethnicity* and has often caused confusion when people have used *race* to describe any group of people they choose. To call, for example, Americans,

---

[7] Merriam-Webster.com, s.v. "ethnic".

[8] Roger Ballard, "Race, Ethnicity and Culture," *New Directions in Sociology* (June 2002): 1-44.

[9] Encyclopædia Britannica Online, s.v. "race".

[10] George Yancey, *One Body, One Spirit: Principles of Successful Multiracial Churches* (Downers Grove, IL: InterVarsity Press, 2003), under "Defining Multiracial Congregations," Kindle.

Frenchman, Catholics, and Jews "races" would be incorrect.[11] The United Nations recommends eschewing the word *race* altogether in favor of the term *ethnic groups.*

> National, religious, geographic, linguistic and cultural groups do not necessarily coincide with racial groups; and the cultural traits of such groups have no demonstrated genetic connection with racial traits. Because serious errors of this kind are habitually committed when the term "race" is used in popular parlance, it would be better when speaking of human races to drop the term "race" altogether and speak of ethnic groups.[12]

From a scriptural standpoint, the word *ethnic* is derived from the Greek word, *ethnos,* which means "nation" or "mankind."[13] In Acts 17:26, Paul recounts the biblical view of the origin of man, and the word *ethnos* is used: "From one man he made every nation (*ethnos*) of men, that they should inhabit the whole earth; and he determined the times set for them and the exact places where they should live."[14] Therefore, from the Creation account and indeed from God's perspective, there is only one race, the human race, which is descended from Adam, with all the wonder and baggage that this implies.

Still, ethnicity does seem to be a topic open to much debate and discussion, taken in light of recent events within the United States. Questions of ethnic fluidity have been raised by the actions of people

---

[11] A. Metraux, "United Nations Economic and Security Council, Statement by Experts on Problems of Race," *American Anthropologist* 53, no. 1 (1951): 142.

[12] Ibid., 142-143.

[13] W. E. Vine, *An Expository Dictionary of New Testament Words* (Nashville, TN: Thomas Nelson, Inc., 1985), 465.

[14] New International Version is used here and for all other references unless otherwise noted.

such as Rachel Dolezal who, while biologically of Anglo-European decent, posed as African American for many years, even to the point of becoming the head of the Spokane, Washington NAACP, a position traditionally held by an African-American.[15] While it is not within the scope of this book to render an opinion on such matters, it does raise questions about culture and ethnicity. Can a church (or youth group) be culturally diverse yet ethnically homogenous? Can a church (or youth group) be culturally homogenous yet ethnically diverse? As to the first question, can a church be culturally diverse yet ethnically homogenous; I believe the answer is yes. At VCC, for example, two of our congregations are African. One is an English-speaking congregation that draws on African immigrants from countries such as Kenya, Nigeria, Zimbabwe, and Ghana, while the other is a French-speaking congregation whose members consist of Christians from countries such as Cameroon, Ivory Coast, and Chad. While each congregation shares a common language and ethnicity, their cultures are very diverse. Examples of these types of congregations (and youth groups) can be found in the United States among Latino churches where Latinos from different countries (Honduras, Mexico, Guatemala) may gather together for corporate worship in Spanish, yet each celebrate and originate from different cultures.

As to the second question, can a church be culturally homogenous yet ethnically diverse? The answer is a resounding…maybe. In large cities with vast immigrant populations, it is quite possible as the original immigrants' children assimilate with the local culture. Children from African immigrants who came to Vienna (or New York or Chicago) tend to adapt to their new culture faster than their parents, and the grandchildren even more so. Therefore, in a church or youth group, it is possible to have a mix of ethnicities who all share a common culture, (e.g., American, Austrian, etc.). Some might say that the children of

---

[15] Sam Frizell, "Rachel Dolezal: I Was Born White," *Time*, November 2, 2015.

African immigrants would identify as African-American when coming to the United States; however, some research has indicated that while in the 1970s, second-generation Caribbean blacks were pressured "to become not so much American, but Afro-American,"[16] this has changed. Recent research on black West-Indian youth points toward the youth as self-identifying as American or as ethnic Americans, with a minority maintaining their immigrant identity.

A few years ago, I was the guest speaker at a church in Alabama. After the service, I was approached by a young woman from Nigeria who had recently immigrated to the United States with her two teenage sons. As our conversation progressed, she mentioned that her sons, ages 13 and 15, were experiencing an identity crisis. She explained that her sons felt pressured by some to conform to the African-American culture, yet they did not feel like they "fit" that culture. The young men explained to their mom, "We don't dress, or talk like African-Americans, and we certainly don't like that style of music." Then they asked their mother, "Mom, if we are not African-American… what are we?" The mother, knowing that I worked with students in similar circumstances in Europe, looked at me with an expression of loss on her face and asked, "What do I tell them?" I paused for a moment to frame my answer, "Tell them they are Nigerian-American." Her eyes grew wide and a smile spread across her face as she comprehended my response. In one sense of the word, her children were African-American; that is people of African descent residing in America, however in the sense of belonging to the African-American subculture—the teenagers recognized that they did not fit into that cultural designation. Like many immigrants of different ethnicities, they find themselves identifying simply as American or as Ethnic Americans.

---

[16] Mary Waters, "Ethnic and Racial Identities of Second-Generation Black Immigrants in New York City," *International Migration Review* 28, no. 4 (1994): 800.

Multiethnic Church

Definitions of a Multiethnic Church (MEC) vary. In his book, *One New People: Models for Developing a Multiethnic Church*, Manuel Ortiz includes five different definitions from five multiethnic church experts. While all five definitions have similarities, each definition has its subtle nuances and differences. All agree that a multiethnic church is a church where different ethnic groups come together in a spirit of unity to worship as one, so that the casual observer cannot simply label the church as black, white, Asian, or Hispanic.[17] Some believe that for a church to truly be a MEC, it should contain 20 percent of different ethnic groups to qualify.[18] Examples of this would be a church that is 20 percent white and 80 percent Hispanic or a church that is 20 percent Hispanic, 20 percent Asian, 20 percent black and 40 percent white.

Multicultural Church

While similar to multiethnic churches in many respects, multicultural churches embrace other categories than just ethnicity. The reality is that many multiethnic churches are in fact multicultural churches. Paul Hiebert's definition of a MEC fits perfectly as the definition of a multicultural church (MCC). Hiebert writes that it is

> A church in which there is (1) an attitude and practice of accepting people of all ethnic, class and national origins as equal and fully participating members and ministers in the fellowship of the church and (2) the manifestation of the attitude and

---

[17] Manuel Ortiz, *One New People: Models for Developing a Multiethnic Church* (Downers Grove, IL: IVP Academic, 1996), 149.

[18] For more on this see Ortiz, One New People: Models for Developing a Multiethnic Church, and Yancey, One Body, One Spirit: Principles of Successful Multiracial Churches.

practice by the involvement of people from different ethnic, social and national communities as members in the church.[19]

Some, like Pastor Mark DeYmaz, prefer to use the term multiethnic over multicultural as to avoid confusion with the views of multiculturalism found on many university campuses.[20] For similar reasons, George Yancey prefers not to use the term, "multicultural," but rather prefers the term, "multiracial," to describe the types of youth ministries we will be describing in this book. However, Yancey does concede that many of the churches that he labels as multiethnic could also correctly be identified as multicultural.[21]

Healthy Multicultural Youth Ministry

Decades ago, there was a phenomenon in some churches called "Volley Ball" youth ministry. Large crowds of youth would gather every week to participate in social and sporting events, with little or no spiritual development. Large numbers of teenagers do not necessarily mean a healthy youth group.[22] While there is no doubt that enjoying time with friends and social interaction are important in church-based youth

---

[19] Ortiz, *One New People*, 149.

[20] Mark DeYmaz, *Building a Healthy Multi-Ethnic Church* (San Francisco, CA: John Wiley & Sons, 2007), 61, Kindle.

[21] Yancey, *One Body, One Spirit*, under "Defining Multiracial Congregations," Kindle.

[22] Some research indicates that the modal average size of a youth group globally is 20-40 students. North America and the U.K. tend to have larger youth groups (80-150), with Asia and Latin America being second (40-80). Africa, Australia, New Zealand, and Continental Europe tend to be smaller (10-20), and India has the fewest numbers (under 10). For more information, see Len Kageler, "A Cross National Analysis of Church Based Youth Ministries," *The Journal of Youth Ministry* 8, no. 2 (2010): 49-69.

ministry,[23] spiritual growth is critical; otherwise, the group is just a social club. For the purpose of this book, a healthy multicultural youth ministry is a youth ministry that follows a "Win, Build, and Send" paradigm, as advocated by Christ in Matthew 4:19: "Come, follow me (Win)," Jesus said, "and I will make you (Build) fishers of men (Send)." The healthy multicultural youth ministry will advocate and promote evangelism of teenagers *across all cultures* and intentionally disciple teenagers so that they grow strong in their faith to be released into ministry to repeat the cycle. This is not to say that they are programmatic in their approach, but rather healthy multicultural youth ministry is relational, holistic, and incarnational.[24] Each part of the Win, Build, and Send model is crucial. To engage in evangelism without making provision for discipleship is like "giving birth and then leaving the baby in the dumpster."[25] Just as Jesus released his disciples into ministry (Matt. 10, Luke 12), healthy youth ministries will also release teenage disciples into ministry. In other words, a healthy youth ministry is a place where teens are transformed into disciples of Christ that make other disciples of Christ.

For the purposes of this book, the term *youth ministry* is being used rather than the term *student ministry*. While both terms are used interchangeably in the North American context of ministry to teenagers, the term *student ministry* may cause some confusion in a European context as student ministry in Europe almost always refers to ministry to university students. Perhaps this is because in Germany and Austria when someone is called a student, it always refers to a university student, while someone in elementary, middle, or high school is called a *schüler*,

---

[23] Len Kageler, "A Cross National Analysis of Church Based Youth Ministries," *The Journal of Youth Ministry* 8, no. 2 (2010): 56.

[24] Terry D. Linhart and David Livermore, *Global Youth Ministry*, Under "Global Youth Ministry is Holistic," Kindle.

[25] Plueddemann, Leading across Cultures, 53.

which is derived from the German word, *schule* or school. Indeed, even the word *youth* can have different definitions depending upon the culture. In Spain, *jovenes* ("youth" or "young people") could include unmarried people into their late twenties, while in the United States youth consists of those typically between 12 or 13 and 18 years of age. In India, youth can include people up to 35 years old, and still other cultures do not have a word that means "adolescence."[26] So as to avoid any confusion between ministry targeting university students and ministry focusing on teenagers, the term *youth ministry* will be used.

---

[26] Terry D. Linhart and David Livermore, *Global Youth Ministry*, Under "The Growth of Global Youth Ministry," Kindle.

Chapter 3

——◦◦——

Multicultural Ministry in the Bible

What does the Bible say about multicultural ministry? Contrary to what some may believe, the Bible is not silent on the topic. While there are differences in the way multicultural ministry was carried out in the Old and New Testaments, without a doubt God's love and concern for all *ethnos* is clearly seen. By examining the scriptures, a pattern begins to emerge from the texts.

Old Testament

While some may be inclined to believe that the *Missio Dei* (Mission of God) in the Old Testament was exclusively to the Jews, they would be mistaken. Although it is accurate to say that, for the most part, the *Missio Dei* was carried out in a centripetal manner, it was open to those outside of Israel. Centripetal, in this context, refers to the mission of God as being passive in that it drew people in from outside of Israel to a central point (such as the tabernacle or the temple in Jerusalem) where certain events influenced outsiders to come and seek God.[1] The centripetal (drawing in) nature of the *Missio Dei* is evident in several places in the

---

[1] J. Kevin Livingston, Missiology of the Road, A: Early Perspectives in David Bosch's Theology of Mission and Evangelism (Cambridge, UK: James Clarke & Co, 2014), 175.

Old Testament. After the supernatural plagues devastated Egypt and the Jews left the country, Exodus records that "Many other people went up with them…" (Exod. 12:38). In other words, many Egyptians and non-Jews participated in the Exodus and became a part of the Jewish community.

Further reading of the Old Testament reveals mechanisms in place that would allow foreigners to become part of the Jewish faith, such as those found in 2 Chronicles 6:32-33. In addition, many examples exist in which groups of people and individuals were drawn to the Jewish faith due to the centripetal nature of the *Missio Dei*. One such group example is found in Esther 8:17: "In every province and in every city, wherever the edict of the king went, there was joy and gladness among the Jews, with feasting and celebrating. And many people of other nationalities became Jews because fear of the Jews had seized them." Examples of individuals who responded to the centripetal nature of the mission of God include Naaman the Leper (2 Kings 5:15-19), Rahab (Josh. 6:25), and Ruth (Ruth 1:16). It is interesting to note that two of these examples, Rahab and Ruth, who may have not been accepted by some during their lifetime due to their status as foreigners, became ancestors of Jesus (Matt. 1:5).

New Testament

While the *Missio Dei* in the Old Testament was centripetal and more passive, the Mission of God in the New Testament is seen as centrifugal or active. Centrifugal carries the connotation of people being sent out from a central point, crossing boundaries to carry out the *Missio Dei*.[2] The centrifugal nature of the New Testament is clearly seen in the gospel of Mark: "He (Jesus) said to them, 'Go into all the world and preach the

---

[2] Livingston, *Missiology of the Road*, 175.

good news to all creation"' (Mark 16:15), and again in Luke, "and repentance and forgiveness of sins will be preached in his name to all nations, beginning at Jerusalem" (Luke 24:47). It is important to note that "all nations" refers to all *ethnos*, or all mankind. Throughout the New Testament, Jesus sent His disciples out crossing boundaries of country, language, ethnicity, and culture. More than that, Jesus modeled this for His disciples. In His encounter with the Samaritan woman (John 4), for example, Jesus crosses cultural, ethnic, gender, societal, and religious boundaries to reach her with the gospel.

Acts 2 records that at the birth of the New Testament Church on the day of Pentecost, there were "God-fearing Jews from every nation under heaven" (Acts 2:5). Some of the many different cultures that were represented are described in following verses: "Parthians, Medes and Elamites; residents of Mesopotamia, Judea and Cappadocia, Pontus and Asia, Phrygia and Pamphylia, Egypt and the parts of Libya near Cyrene; visitors from Rome (both Jews and converts to Judaism); Cretans and Arabs" (Acts 2:9-11). With over 3000 people responding to Peter's message and being baptized, it is probable that many were from cultural and ethnic backgrounds different from those of the disciples. Granted the vast majority of these new believers were probably Jews and converts to Judaism (Acts 2:11), but the cultural differences became evident in the Early Church's growing pains.

One of the first internal crises faced by the Early Church had, at its roots, a cultural component. The Grecian Jews complained against the Hebraic Jews, claiming that the Grecian widows were being neglected during the daily food distribution. Wisely, the disciples asked the body to resolve this by appointing seven men to oversee the distribution. The only qualification that the disciples required of these men was that they be "full of the Spirit and wisdom" (Acts 6:3). The seven men that were selected all had Greek names, and one (Nicolas) was a convert to

Judaism. It is most likely that these men were chosen from the Grecian Jews.[3]

Crossing ethnic and cultural barriers did not seem to be much of a problem for the Early Church, as long as the people they were reaching were Jews. Philip's encounter with the Ethiopian official in Acts 8 did not seem to bother anyone in the Early Church as much as Peter's encounter with Cornelius did (Acts 10). It took supernatural intervention for the disciples to begin to see that when Jesus said to go to all *ethnos*, He really meant everyone--even the Gentiles. The hand of the Lord can be seen moving powerfully in the conversion of Cornelius and his household. First, an angel appears to Cornelius, instructing him to send men to bring Peter to him. The next day, the Lord gives Peter three visions to prepare his heart for what was about to come. At the conclusion of the final vision, the men sent by Cornelius arrive, and Peter receives another word from the Lord, instructing him to go with the men. After arriving at Cornelius's house, Peter reminds those who were assembled that it was against the Jewish law for him to be there, but God had shown him that he should not "call any man impure or unclean" (Acts 10:28). Then, as Peter is sharing the gospel with those who had been gathered, an amazing thing happens: "The Holy Spirit came upon all who heard the message" (Acts 10:44). As a result, Peter took the unusual step of baptizing the new Gentile believers.

These events caused no small uproar in Jerusalem, where Peter was called to account for his actions. Acts 11:2 recounts that "when Peter went up to Jerusalem, the circumcised believers criticized him." The word *criticized* in Greek is *diakrino*, which means "to contend with" or "to separate oneself from," as the Archangel Michael contended with Satan (Jude 3), indicating that there was no small disagreement about Peter's

---

[3] Ralph W. Harris, ed., *The Complete Biblical Library: New Testament Study Bible; Acts* (Chicago, IL: R.R. Donnelley and Sons, 1991), 137.

20

behavior.[4] Only after Peter, who had wisely brought witnesses,[5] explained that it was at the supernatural direction of the Lord that they went to Cornelius's house and the miraculous outpouring of the Holy Spirit happened, did the circumcised believers somewhat reluctantly admit, "So then, God has granted even the Gentiles repentance unto life" (Acts 11:18). One commentary remarks as follows:

> Though the Jerusalem apostles and believers accepted the fact that Gentiles in Caesarea were saved and had become part of the church, it did not excite them very much. There was no rush to go out and win more Gentiles to the Lord. Even Peter continued to consider his ministry as primarily to the "circumcision" (to the Jews) and kept ministering on most occasions to Jews only.[6]

It was not until the Apostle Paul began to make inroads into Gentile territory that a deliberate effort was made to reach all *ethnos*, regardless of whether they were Jew or Gentile. Indeed, many of the letters written to these multicultural congregations reinforced the idea that the new believers did not need to be circumcised or follow the Jewish law. Not wanting to make the new Gentile converts' lives difficult, the Apostles sent instructions to the new believers in the church at Antioch: "Instead we should write to them, telling them to abstain from food polluted by idols, from sexual immorality, from the meat of strangled animals and from blood."[7] In other words, they were welcoming the Gentiles into the body of Christ and encouraging them to live holy lives.

---

[4] Vine, Expository Dictionary, 125.

[5] See Acts 10:23 and Acts 11:12 for more information.

[6] Harris, Complete Biblical Library: Acts, 277.

[7] This instruction is found in Acts 15:20 and also repeated in Acts 15:29 (NIV).

Other examples of the multicultural composition of the Early Church abound. One final illustration is the makeup of the believers in the church at Antioch who were set apart to serve in missions (Acts 13). Barnabas was from Cyprus (Acts 4:36) while Simeon called Niger was likely from Africa.[8] Lucius was from Cyrene, a Greek colony in North Africa, while Manaen was the foster brother of Herod Antipas, the same Herod who had John the Baptist executed. Manaen was raised in the palace, and he was likely well-educated and obviously from the upper class of society.[9] Finally, there was Saul from Tarsus (Acts 9:11). It is not surprising, considering his background, that Saul (also called Paul; Acts 13:9), who was raised in the Greek culture of Tarsus, was born a Roman citizen (Acts 22:28), and was raised in the Jewish faith as the son of a Pharisee (Acts 23:6), should be called as the Apostle to the Gentiles. It was Paul's admonition to the Colossians that encouraged them that truly "there is no Greek or Jew, circumcised or uncircumcised, barbarian, Scythian, slave or free, but Christ is all, and is in all" (Col. 3:11-15). Indeed, a close examination of the Book of Acts will reveal that there are no mono-cultural churches listed. Unfortunately, many Christians in the United States believe "make disciples of all nations" is something only missionaries do.[10]

When we compare the multicultural paradigm of the church in Acts with the scene in Heaven recorded in Revelation 7:9-10, the pattern becomes clear:

> After this I looked and there before me was a great multitude that no one could count, from every nation, tribe, people and

---

[8] Niger means black and this has led some scholars to conclude that Simon was from Africa or of African descent.

[9] Harris, Complete Biblical Library: Acts, 303.

[10] Rodney Woo, *The Color of Church* (Nashville, TN: B&H Publishing Group, 2009), 90.

language, standing before the throne and in front of the Lamb. They were wearing white robes and were holding palm branches in their hands. And they cried out in a loud voice: "Salvation belongs to our God, who sits on the throne, and to the Lamb."

Christian believers from every nation (*ethnos*) are gathered together worshiping in unity. It should be obvious that "God accepts and receives all people regardless of social status, color of skin, level of education or nationality."[11] Equally obvious is the idea that the twenty-first century Christian church should be just as accepting and multicultural.

---

[11] Ibid., 85.

Chapter 4

---∞---

Ethnicity and Culture in the church

D r. Manuel Ortiz, author and professor emeritus at Westminster Theological Seminary, comments about the current multicultural status of the church in America: "In the United States it is still true that Sunday morning at 11 a.m. is the most segregated hour of the week. Black, white, Hispanic and Asian Christians watch each other pour out of their church buildings on street intersections that are often their only common meeting ground."[1] George Yancey agrees with Ortiz's assessment.[2] Yancey's definition of a multiethnic church is a church where no one ethnic group has more than 80 percent of the attendance in a main church service. By this criterion, only about 8 percent of all churches within the United States are multiethnic.[3] It seems that there has been a significant shift away from the multicultural church paradigm that was evident in Scripture. Has the church always been so monocultural? The short answer appears to be no, it has not.

---

[1] Ortiz, *One New People*, 10.

[2] Yancey, *One Body, One Spirit*, under "Introduction," Kindle.

[3] Yancey, *One Body, One Spirit*, under "Defining Multiracial Congregations," Kindle.

History of Monocultural Church Development

During the mid-1800s, virtually every Evangelical Church that existed in the United States encountered some tension over the issue of slavery. In 1837 and again in 1857, the Presbyterian Church split over the issue of slavery. In 1844, the Methodist Episcopal Church divided because of slavery, and then a year later in 1845, the Southern Baptist Convention was formed by Baptist churches in the South that supported the institution of slavery. With all the infighting and division over this issue, it comes as no surprise that there was a mass exodus of blacks from the white churches.[4] It was not until 150 years later, in 1995, that the Southern Baptist Convention took radical steps toward ethnic reconciliation. The 150th Southern Baptist Convention in Atlanta, Georgia, passed a resolution of racial reconciliation. Among other things, the resolution acknowledged that the Convention was "hindered from the beginning by the role that slavery played in the formation of the Southern Baptists."[5] The resolution also calls on the Convention to "lament and repudiate"[6] evil such as slavery, and calls on its members as a body to repent and apologize to African-Americans for the sin of racism. Finally, the resolution called on its members to actively pursue reconciliation, and to eliminate racism while fulfilling the Great Commission.[7] In June 2012, the Southern Baptist Convention elected Fred Luter, Jr., an African-American, as its president. Multiracial churches existed in the United States before the Civil War in the face of prejudice, mistreatment, and oppression of African Americans

---

[4] Woo, The Color of Church, 80.

[5] "Resolution on Racial Reconciliation on the 150th Anniversary of the Southern Baptist Convention," Southern Baptist Convention.

[6] Ibid.

[7] Ibid.

multiracial churches still exists. "Their historical existence proves that we can overcome the racial barriers that work against their creation today."[8]

Other denominations that were not in existence until after the Civil War were also impacted negatively by the effects of racism that permeated society at the time of their founding. One such example is the Assemblies of God. The founding of the Assemblies of God has its roots in Topeka, Kansas and was propelled by Azusa Street revival in 1906, when an African-American preacher, William J. Seymour, became the pastor at a church in Los Angeles. It was not long before the revival taking place at his church became known nationwide, with people from all over the United States attending.[9] One of the extraordinary characteristics of the Azusa Street revival was its multicultural makeup. People from different cultural and ethnic backgrounds came together in a spirit of unity. Dr. Gary McGee, professor of Church History at the Assemblies of God Theological Seminary, writes,

> African-Americans, Latinos, whites, and others prayed and sang together, creating a dimension of spiritual unity and equality, almost unprecedented for the time. It allowed men, women, and children to celebrate their unity in Christ and participate as led by the Spirit. Indeed, so unusual was the mixture of blacks and whites, that (Frank) Bartleman enthusiastically exclaimed, "The color line was washed away in the blood." He meant that in the sanctifying work of the Holy Spirit, the sin of racial prejudice had been removed by the cleansing blood of Jesus Christ.[10]

---

[8] Yancey, *One Body, One Spirit*, under "The Present Reality," Kindle.

[9] Paul Chappell, "Healing Movements," in *The Dictionary of Pentecostal and Charismatic Movements*, ed. Stanley Burgess and Gary McGee (Grand Rapids, MI: Zondervan, 1988), 368.

[10] Gary McGee, "William J. Seymour and the Azusa Street Revival," *Enrichment Journal* (Fall 1999): 2.

At one of the Azusa street revival services was a young man named E. S. Williams who would later become a General Superintendent of the Assemblies of God. Prior to the founding of the Assemblies of God (AG) in 1914, blacks and whites would worship together in Pentecostal churches; however, by 1913, pressure from society and Jim Crow laws affected these churches. In 1917, the officers of the Assemblies of God refused to commission Alexander Howard, an African-American, as a missionary to Liberia. They told Howard that "it was not God's will to send a colored person to do missions work in Africa."[11] This eventually led many African-American Pentecostals to join the newly formed United Pentecostal Council of the Assemblies of God (UPCAG). The problems with race within the Assemblies of God intensified to the point that in 1939, the Assemblies of God created policies that would not allow African-Americans to be ordained. This policy continued until 1962, when it was eventually repealed; however, the ethnic rift remained for almost 100 years.[12]

In June 2010, the newly elected International Presiding Elder of the UPCAG wrote a letter to the General Superintendent of the Assemblies of God, Dr. George Wood. In part, the letter read,

> Accept greetings in the name of our wonderful Lord and Savior Jesus Christ. My name is Thomas A. Barclay, and I recently was elected as the International Presiding Elder of the United Pentecostal Council of the Assemblies of God, Inc. I have always been interested in reunifying our two fellowships. ... The issues which separated us from the Assemblies of God in 1919 are no

---

[11] Scott Harrup, "A Larger Family," *The Pentecostal Evangel*, January 16, 2011.

[12] Ibid.

longer valid. I am feeling compelled by the Lord to make the effort to end this separation.[13]

This initiative of reconciliation started by Barclay culminated in a plan of cooperative affiliation whereby UPCAG churches and AG would work together to "carry out the Great Commission as given by Jesus Christ our Lord."[14] This includes participation in world missions (the very thing that caused the division) as well as shared resources in youth, children's, and compassion ministries. It is curious that it took so long to reconcile this schism since over 40 percent of current Assemblies of God membership is made up of ethnic minorities.[15]

Current Status of the Church

Although major breakthroughs have occurred in reconciliation between ethnic groups within some of the denominations in the United States, research continues to suggest that the churches are mostly monochromatic. The American Congregational Giving Study showed that in 1993, 42.9 percent of the surveyed churches did not have one member of another ethnic group attending. Furthermore while white Anglo-Americans made up 74.4 percent of the population of the United States, they represented over 90 percent of the members of the churches.[16] If using the 80/20 definition of a multiethnic church (where

---

[13] Thomas Barclay, quoted in Scott Harrup, "A Larger Family," *The Pentecostal Evangel*, January 16, 2011, 1.

[14] "Cooperative Fellowship Agreement between United Pentecostal Council of the Assemblies of God and Assemblies of God," February 14, 2014.

[15] "A Vital Step Forward: The AG and UPCAG Unite," AG News, February 14, 2014.

[16] Kevin D. Dougherty, "How Monochromatic Is Church Membership? Racial-Ethnic Diversity in Religious Community," *Sociology of Religion* 64, no. 1 (2003): 65-85.

at least 20 percent of the church is from a different ethnic group than the majority 80 percent), only 7.5 percent of all churches in the United States can be described as multiethnic churches.[17] However, research suggests that progress is being made in the area of culturally and ethnically diverse churches, two of the most ethnically inclusive groups being the Roman Catholic Church and the Assemblies of God. [18]

Monoethnic churches are not exclusive to the United States; indeed, they can be found all over the world, especially in Europe. Benjamin Brestak, the National Youth Director of Shake Youth for *Freie Christengemeinde Österreich* (Free Christian Churches of Austria, or FCGÖ), spoke about the situation in Austria. The FCGÖ is, for the most part, ethnically homogenous, with those of European descent making up the majority of its members. However, some of the churches in the FCGÖ are quite culturally diverse, with pastors and members who originate from other parts of Europe (e.g., Italy, Romania, Hungary, and Slovakia). [19] In many ways, this mirrors the situation in the United States, where we can find people in churches who share the same ethnic heritage (Anglo-European) but share different cultural backgrounds (Italian, Irish, German, and Swedish). Thus, while many of the FCGÖ churches are rich in cultural diversity, there are very few churches, if any, that are ethnically diverse. It is important to note that this evaluation was based on the 80/20 definition of a multiethnic church.

---

[17] DeYmaz, Healthy Multi-Ethnic Church, 4.

[18] Dougherty, "Monochromatic Church Membership," 65-85.

[19] Benjamin Brestak, interview by author, Vienna, Austria, February 8, 2016.

Changes in Hispanic Churches

Perhaps one transformation that foreshadows the opportunities available to churches to reach out to all cultures is a phenomenon taking place in some large Latino churches in the United States. Traditionally, Latino churches conduct their worship services in Spanish, but recent trends in immigration and language began to cause a momentum loss in the traditional Latino worship services. In 2005, 60 percent of the Hispanics in the United States were born there.[20] In addition, English is becoming the *Lingua Franca* among Hispanics, who report that over 68 percent speak English only in their homes or have a high degree of fluency.[21]

Seeing these trends impacting the local church has led some pastors to take the radical, yet logical, step of transitioning from a Spanish-speaking church to a bilingual Spanish-and-English-speaking church. Two such churches are New Life Covenant Ministries with Pastor Wilfredo de Jesus in Chicago, and *Iglesia del Redentor* (Church of the Redeemer) with Pastor Aureliano Flores in Baldwin Park, California.[22] Both pastors felt this paradigm shift was necessary for two primary reasons: (1) to reach their children and youth who were becoming less proficient in Spanish and who preferred to attend English-speaking services, and (2) to serve and evangelize the surrounding community.[23]

---

[20] Daniel Rodriguez, "Hispanic Ministry Where Language Is No Barrier," *Great Commission Research Journal* 1, no. 2 (Winter 2010): 189-201.

[21] Gustavo Lopez and Eileen Patten, "The Impact of Slowing Immigration: Foreign-Born Share Falls Among 14 Largest U.S. Hispanic Origin Groups," Pew Research Center Hispanic Trends, September 15, 2015.

[22] Rodriguez, "Hispanic Ministry," 192-195.

[23] Ibid., 189-201.

Another church that made the transition from the traditional Latino service to a bilingual service is *La Iglesia Alpha y Omega* (Alpha and Omega Church) in Miami, Florida, led by Pastor Alberto Delgado. When parishioners asked why the church needed to transition to the new model, Delgado replied, "If we do not adjust (our approach) we run the risk of losing our children and grandchildren to the world."[24] Now over four hundred youth attend the weekly youth services at *La Iglesia Alpha y Omega*. The language is a mix of English and Spanish, and the worship consists of popular contemporary music and salsa style worship.[25]

Cultural and Ethnic Diversity on the Rise

The face of the United States (as well as Europe) is quickly changing. The pastors at New Life Covenant Ministries, *Iglesia del Redentor*, and *La Iglesia Alpha y Omega* have recognized this and have adjusted their ministry to serve not only those cultures that they traditionally reached with the Gospel, but also the lost of other cultures as well. Prudent pastors and youth pastors should reflect on their example and become like the men from Issachar "who understood the times and knew what Israel should do" (1 Chr. 12:32). By the year 2065, no one ethnic group will be the majority within the United States. The Pew Research Center calculates that by 2065, 46 percent of the population will be White non-Hispanic (down from 62 percent), 24 percent will be Hispanic (up from 18 percent), 14 percent will be Asian (up from 6 percent) and 13 percent will be Black (up from 12 percent).[26] While the Hispanic population will

---

[24] Ibid., 198.

[25] Ibid., 196.

[26] D'Vera Cohn, "Future Immigration Will Change the Face of America by 2065," Pew Research Center, October 5, 2015.

be the second largest population in the U.S. by 2065, most of this growth is due to birth rather than immigration. The largest immigrant group is projected to be Asians, who will make up 38 percent of the foreign-born population.[27]

The United States is not the only country that faces a massive population shift. In 2015, Germany expected to receive over 1.5 million immigrants and refugees.[28] The vast majorities of these displaced people are applying for asylum and look to be in Europe long term. Of special note to those interested in youth ministry is that 26.4 percent of the immigrants seeking asylum in Europe are under eighteen years old.[29] Already churches and missions organization are ministering to and serving these new arrivals by providing food, shelter, clothing, and other resources, and the fruit of their labor is being seen in the harvest. In a two-week period, over thirty people from the Middle East converted to Christianity after hearing the Gospel experiencing the love of Christ through the local church, and all thirty converts testified about having a dream or vision of Jesus. Among these converts are teenagers who are now being integrated into the church and into discipleship programs to strengthen their newly found faith.

There are challenges that accompany these changes, to be sure. Within the United States, the reaction to immigrants is mixed; half of American adults believe that immigrants are making crime and the

---

[27] Pew Research Center, "Modern Immigration Wave Brings 59 Million to U.S., Driving Population Growth and Change through 2065: Views of Immigration's Impact on U.S. Society Mixed" (Washington, DC: Pew Research Center, 2015), 13, PDF.

[28] Michelle Martin, "Patrols to Block Expected 1.5 Million Refugees Flooding across Europe," *Sydney Morning Herald*, October 5, 2015.

[29] Drew DeSliver, "Refugee Surge Brings Youth to an Aging Europe," Pew Research Center, October 8, 2015.

economy worse, yet about the same number claim that immigrants are making art, music, and food better.[30] In Europe, some countries have closed their borders in an attempt to halt the flow of immigrants, while other countries have welcomed them with open arms. As of this writing, tensions have grown in parts of Europe as groups of immigrant men have reportedly assaulted women, and anti-immigrant protests have turned violent.[31] Yet with these challenges also come opportunities to minister to the teenage immigrants and introduce them to the gospel. Many of these immigrants coming to Europe are from Muslim countries that are traditionally closed to the gospel. Now they find themselves in countries where there is religious freedom, and they are exposed to the gospel for the first time. Churches and missions organizations are seeing many of these immigrants converting to Christianity, and some missiologist believe that more Muslims are coming to Christ in Europe than in any other region of the world. Since over 25 percent of all the new immigrants are children and teens, it is reasonable to surmise that many teenagers and children are now Christ followers. What better way is there to disciple these new teens than by integrating them into existing churches and youth ministries? Whether in the United States or in Europe, the principle is the same--there is an incredible opportunity to win teenagers to Christ, disciple them into strong believers, and to release them back into ministry.

---

[30] Pew Research Center, "Modern Immigration Wave", 13.

[31] Joseph Nasr and Matthias Inverardi, "Anti-Migrant Protest Turns Violent as German Welcome Cools," Reuters, January 9, 2016.

Chapter 5

---oo---

New Opportunities

Whether in North America, Europe, or other parts of the world, it is the goal of healthy youth ministries to win teenagers to Christ, build them into disciples, and then release them into ministry—and not just teenagers who share the same culture as the church or youth leader, but all *ethnos* of teenagers. George Yancey has identified several advantages of a multiethnic church that should be applicable to a multicultural youth ministry. These include "reaching multiracial communities, racial reconciliation, demonstrating racial unity as a witness, and obedience to God."[1] While some would argue that establishing multicultural youth ministry would be more difficult than a monocultural youth ministry due to the inherent conflict in multicultural churches, Yancey's research did not find *any* evidence that that conflict was higher in multicultural churches than monocultural churches.[2] In some respects, establishing a multicultural youth ministry should not be as difficult as some would suppose, due to two circumstances: millennials' attitudes toward interethnic relationships, and commonalties in youth ministry globally.

---

[1] Yancey, *One Body, One Spirit*, under "Advantages of Multiracial Churches," Kindle.

[2] Yancey, *One Body, One Spirit*, under "Church Growth Arguments," Kindle.

Teenagers, Ethnicity, and Culture

The Pew Research Center has discovered that while all generations have experienced an increase in support for interethnic dating and marriages, the highest support comes from Millennials, with 93 percent of 18 to 29-year-olds agreeing with the statement, "I think it is all right for blacks and whites to date each other."[3] Further Pew research indicates that while older adults are less likely to have cross-ethnic friendships, over half of Millennials do.[4] This is likely caused by the Propinquity Effect,[5] which takes place at school. As cultural and ethnic diversity increase at school, and by extension, within youth ministries, we are likely to see even more cross-cultural and cross-ethnic friendships develop.[6] A youth group is a place where many teenagers discover some of the closest friends they will ever have, and combining teenagers' openness to multiethnic friendships and the bonding that can take place in youth groups due in part to the Propinquity Effect, a multicultural youth group can expose teens to different cultures and create opportunities for them to build relationships with other teenagers from other cultural and ethnic backgrounds.[7] So not only does a multicultural youth group meet

---

[3] "Almost All Millennials Accept Interracial Dating and Marriage," Pew Research Center, February 1, 2010.

[4] Ibid.

[5] The Propinquity Effect is a phenomenon whereby people who associate together regularly tend to develop friendships or romantic relationships.

[6] Lincoln Quillian and Mary E. Campbell, "Beyond Black and White: The Present and Future of Multiracial Friendship Segregation," *American Sociological Review* 68 (2003): 540-66.

[7] Arturo Lucero and Robert Weaver, "Building Healthy Relationships in a Multi-Ethnic Congregation with No Ethnic Majority: A Case Study of Sunrise Church," *Great Commission Research Journal* 2, no. 2 (Winter 2011): 188.

Yancey's ideals concerning multiracial (multiethnic) churches of reaching multicultural communities, demonstrating ethnic unity, and obeying God's Word, but it can also provide a vehicle through which ethnic reconciliation can take place.

Global Commonalities in Youth Ministry

There has been a global youth population explosion, approximately half of the worldwide population now being under the age of 25, with the highest proportions of young people being in developing nations.[8] Global youth ministry has also surged, thanks in part to the prevalence of English as a common language, ease and relative safety of travel, and the development of short-term mission trips.[9] Youth ministry resources that were once difficult, if not virtually impossible, to find in different parts of the world are now available to anyone with a connection to the internet. Resources such as Youth Specialties, Youthwork magazine and website, and *Purpose Driven Youth Ministry* by Doug Fields are some of the most utilized, locally and globally.[10]

Even with vast cultural differences across the planet, some commonalities exist in global youth ministry. In *A Cross National Analysis of Church Based Youth Ministries*, Len Kageler found that youth pastors and leaders on all continents shared the same joys and frustrations of youth ministry. The following are the joys of youth ministry that most Christian

---

[8] Linda Herrera, "What's New about Youth?" *Development and Change* 37, no. 6 (2006): 1425-34.

[9] Linhart and Livermore, *Global Youth Ministry*, Under "The Growth of Global Youth Ministry," Kindle.

[10] Kageler, "Cross National Analysis," 49-69.

youth workers will identify with, no matter their geographic location or cultural background:

- Africa: Seeing youth "get it." Worshipping with youth.
- South Africa: Youth on fire for God! Authentic worship.
- Australia/New Zealand: Personal relationships with youth. Youth being passionate for God.
- India: Doing youth conferences. Affirming youth when they do right.
- Asia: Spending time with youth. Watching youth worship.
- Continental Europe: Seeing answered prayer. Being part of a team.
- UK: Seeing youth mature in Christ. Developing leaders.
- South/Central America: Seeing youth delight in God. Worshipping with youth.
- North America: Seeing youth embrace spirituality. Helping volunteers grow in ministry.[11]

Just as the joys of youth ministry are shared globally among youth leaders, so too are the frustrations. It is worth noting that all areas, with the exception of India, cited the lack of financial resources.[12]

- Africa: Arrogant youth. When a young person whom I've discipled turns away.
- South Africa: Church conflict. Adults not valuing youth.
- Australia/New Zealand: The view that YM is just keeping kids "safe" and attending mass. Youth dropping out at age 18.

---

[11] Ibid., 64.

[12] Ibid.

- India: Some see youth ministry as "lesser" form of ministry. Criticism (from adults) when I use movie clips in my teaching.
- Asia: Church bureaucracy!!! Time pressures.
- Continental Europe: Youth choosing sports and music over church involvement. Old people don't understand the needs of youth.
- UK: Lack of church's willingness to change. Not enough time to do the ministry and have a good family.
- South/Central America: Lack of facilities for our meetings. Seeing youth turn away that I've prayed for and spent time with.
- North America: Inconsistent attendance. Lack of volunteers.[13]

It cannot be stated strongly enough that just because there are commonalties in youth ministry globally indicating that culture does not matter, indeed it does! Culture determines not only how something is done, but also *why* it is done in a particular way. A successful youth leader in Mobile, Alabama, may have the opposite results if he or she were to use the same methods in Sofia, Bulgaria, or rural India. Likewise, a successful youth leader from Lagos, Nigeria, would likely suffer similar failure using Nigerian pedagogy in Two Egg, Florida, or Madrid, Spain.

Therefore, since youth are more inclined to cross ethnic and cultural boundaries to form friendships, and since multicultural ministry is biblical and fully realizes the *Missio Dei*, and since there is strong evidence that youth ministry shares many of the same joys and frustrations across the globe, what then are characteristics that should be present in a healthy multicultural youth ministry?

---

[13] Ibid., 64-65.

Reflection Questions

The purposes of the following questions are to help you think critically and creatively about assessing your current ministry paradigm and how you can begin to reach different cultures and ethnicities.

- What is the history of your denomination or movement as it relates to other ethnicities and cultures? How has this impacted the ethnic/cultural makeup of your denomination or movement?

- What is the history of your local church as it relates to other ethnicities and cultures? How has this impacted the ethnic/cultural makeup of your church?

- Using the 80/20 ratio as a standard, is your church a multicultural or multiethnic church? How does this compare to the youth ministry?

- What are the demographic percentages of your community as it relates to ethnicities and culture? Are these percentages represented in your church/ youth group?

- As in the orchard illustration, has your church / youth group only been focused on one type of fruit or have you been focusing on the entire harvest?

- After reading about some of the global joys and frustrations in youth ministry, what surprised you the most? Why?

- What are some ways that you might leverage the global commonalties in youth ministry to reach youth from different cultures and ethnicities with the gospel?

Now What?

Consider doing the following.

- Contact the pastor or youth pastor of a church that is ethnically different from you and your church. Invite them for coffee and pick their brain about multicultural ministry. Some questions you may consider asking:

  - What is the history of ethnic relations in the community?

  - What is the feeling of ethnic groups toward our church?

  - What can our church do to address issues in the ethnic communities?

  - What does youth ministry look like in their church?

- Conduct a demographic study of the population in your community. Consulting with the church leadership team, determine which group or groups you will engage with first in outreach.

- Visit https://geert-hofstede.com/countries.html and do a comparison with some of the cultures in your area.

Characteristics and understandings

Youth ministry, at the best of times, can be challenging. Not only do youth workers minister to those going through puberty, but they also minister to parents who may be at the end of their mental resources dealing with their teens who are going through puberty. A good youth leader relies on a set of skills that is "truly multidisciplinary: theology, psychology, anthropology, sociology as well as history."[1] The youth worker's goal: to reach as many teens as possible with the gospel, to disciple them, and to release them into ministry. In this, a multicultural youth ministry may help them achieve the first part of this goal. George Yancey found that multicultural churches are more likely to have grown over the past year than monocultural churches, and that on average, multicultural churches are thirty years younger than monocultural congregations.[2] It could be argued that multicultural youth ministry explains this increased rate of growth. The research seems to indicate three broad areas of competencies under which the characteristics and understandings of a healthy multicultural youth ministry lie. These three categories are Leadership, Language and Communication, and Ministry Structures.

---

[1] Len Kageler, "A Cross National Analysis of Church Based Youth Ministries., *The Journal of Youth Ministry* 8, no. 2 (2010): 49.

[2] George Yancey, *One Body, One Spirit: Principles of Successful Multiracial Churches* (Downers Grove, IL: InterVarsity Press, 2003), under "Church Growth Arguments," Kindle.

Chapter 6

Leadership

The overwhelming preponderance of literature in missiology and multiethnic church planting agrees that leadership is one of the key characteristics of a successful multicultural church. "Leadership is the single most important factor of effective church ministry in culturally diverse communities."[1] In virtually all the literature, leadership is the first characteristic to be mentioned. John Maxwell said that "everything rises and falls on leadership."[2] This is also true when it comes to multicultural youth ministry. It is imperative that multicultural youth leaders learn about leadership styles of the cultures among which they work.[3] The leadership characteristics that make someone a strong youth leader in one culture may lead to disaster when trying to lead in a different culture. Culture and leadership expert, Geert Hofstede, beautifully explains it:

---

[1] Sean S. O'Neal, *Bridges to People* (Maitland, FL: Xulon Press, 2007), 225.

[2] John C. Maxwell, The 21 Irrefutable Laws of Leadership: Follow Them and People Will Follow You, rev. ed. (Nashville, TN: Thomas Nelson, 2007), 246.

[3] Elizabeth Drury, "Leading the Mutli-Ethnic Church: Help from New Metaphors and the Leadership Challenge," *Great Commission Research Journal* 2, no. 2 (Winter 2011): 225-26.

Learning to become an effective leader is like learning to play music: Besides talent, it demands persistence and the opportunity to practice. Effective monocultural leaders have learned to play one instrument; they often have proven themselves by a strong drive and quick and firm opinions. Leading in a multicultural and diverse environment is like playing several instruments. It partly calls for different attitudes and skills, restraint in passing judgment and the ability to recognize that familiar tunes may have to be played differently. The very qualities that make someone an effective monocultural leader may make her or him less qualified for a multicultural environment.[4]

Intentionality

A characteristic shared by Mark DeYmaz, Rodney Woo, Wilfredo De Jesus, and missionaries who practice the Indigenous Church Principle[5] is that they are intentional about reaching the lost with the gospel and intentional in crossing cultures doing it. They have taken to heart that it is the *Missio Dei* to reach all *ethnos* with the gospel. In the case of Dr. Woo, who led the transformation of Wilcrest Baptist Church from a declining monocultural church to a thriving multicultural church, he was intentional in getting the church to own the vision of reaching all ethnos. The church formed a task force and used small groups to propagate the vision among the people until the vast majority were on board with that

---

[4] Mary L. Connerley and Paul B. Pedersen, *Leadership in a Diverse and Multicultural Environment: Developing Awareness, Knowledge and Skill* (Thousand Oaks, CA: Sage Publications, 2005), ix, Google Books.

[5] The Indigenous Church Principal posits that churches should be self-led (by indigenous people), self-supporting, and self-propagating. For more information, see Melvin L. Hodges, *The Indigenous Church and the Indigenous Church and the Missionary*, rev. ed. (Springfield, MO: Gospel Publishing House, 2009).

vision.[6] In a similar way, when Pastor De Jesus of New Life Covenant Ministries moved from a monolingual church to a bilingual church that would reach many different cultures, he was intentional about directly addressing the concerns of older Spanish-speaking church members to assure them they would not be marginalized by the new English-speaking majority.[7]

For the youth leaders that desire to have a healthy multicultural youth ministry, this implies that they, too, need to be intentional. They need to be intentional to have the church leadership's support in their endeavor, intentional to patiently lead the church body to embrace the mission of multicultural youth ministry, and intentional in their efforts to reach youth from different cultures. That the youth leader should have an excellent working relationship with the lead pastor goes without saying, and just as the pastors and leaders who transitioned from monocultural churches enlisted the aid of their staff members, church boards, and members of the body, so too the prudent youth leader will enlist the support of the lead pastor before engaging in multicultural youth ministry. Together, they will seek the support of the leadership team and the church body, including the youth leadership team and the youth.

In 2005, I was serving as the youth pastor at First Assembly of God in Panama City, Florida. A man walked into the church offices with a problem. The man had a passion to reach low-income teens of all ethnicities in his community, and he had been driving a bus for one of the local Baptist churches, picking up 25 to 30 teenagers and transporting them to the church for youth service. Apparently, the teens were so ill-

---

[6] Rodney Woo, *The Color of Church* (Nashville, TN: B&H Publishing Group, 2009), 28-29, Kindle.

[7] Daniel Rodriguez, "Hispanic Ministry Where Language Is No Barrier," *Great Commission Research Journal* 1, no. 2 (Winter 2010): 194.

behaved that the church asked the entire group not to come back. The man asked if he could bring the teens to First Assembly. Without hesitating, the lead pastor and I both replied with a resounding "Yes!" The results were a spectacular disaster of Biblical proportions. As soon as the new teenagers began to arrive, parents started to complain about the profane language used by the teens as well as teenagers smoking in the church parking lot. It seemed that all I did on Wednesday nights was patrol the halls to break up the inevitable fist fights. In hindsight, while the pastor and I were in agreement on how to proceed, we had not spent adequate time preparing the church body and the youth group for the change. Nor had we prepared adequate ministry structures that would help win, build, and send those new teens. Several years later, we were able to minister to a multicultural mix of teenagers from the community. This was only possible after being intentional in casting the vision to the entire church, having the leadership and the congregation on board, and having appropriate ministry structures in place.

Everyone sees the world through the lenses of their own culture. For the most part, this serves us well when it is the only culture that we work among. Yet when people begin to develop relationships with other cultures, their own culture can become a prison to them as they assume that their way is the only "right" way of doing things.[8] Those desiring to work with youth in a multicultural context must be intentional about being students of culture. A great temptation for youth workers is to assume that since they have experienced success in one culture, they can just move into multicultural youth ministry without an understanding of the local church culture, the context of ministry, or the culture of the

---

[8] Judith E. Lingenfelter and Sherwood G. Lingenfelter, *Teaching Cross-Culturally: An Incarnation Model for Learning and Teaching* (Grand Rapids, MI: Baker Academic, 2003), 20.

new group they are trying to reach.[9] Some of the greatest tensions in multicultural ministry come from the cultural values that we all hold. "These values are assumed, hidden, subtle and unspoken,"[10] yet everyone from that culture knows them. As will be discussed later under Ministry Structures, understanding characteristics of cultures can alleviate many misunderstandings before they occur. Along with a deep love for God and being led *kata pneuma* (by the Holy Spirit), successful multicultural youth leaders will reveal a love of people and culture.[11]

Finally, a healthy multicultural youth ministry is intentional about getting people out of their comfort zone. This should not be a difficult challenge for most youth leaders. Consider that when an adult comes out of a local store at night and sees a group of teenagers hanging out in the parking lot, most tend to try to avoid the teens. On the other hand, many youth pastors would notice the teenagers in the parking lot and say to themselves (if not aloud) "My people!" and then attempt to connect with them. For the most part, though, crossing ethnic and cultural lines can be uncomfortable for most people. When Wilcrest Baptist Church in Houston, Texas, under the leadership of Dr. Woo, transitioned from a monoethnic, monocultural church to a multiethnic, multicultural church, many within the church body felt tension in leaving their comfort zone. One parishioner remarked, "I definitely forfeited being comfortable as I

---

[9] Terry D. Linhart and David Livermore, *Global Youth Ministry*, under "The Youth of the World," Kindle.

[10] James E. Plueddemann, Leading Across Cultures: Effective Ministry and Mission in the Global Church (Downers Grove, IL: IVP Academic, 2009), 71.

[11] Linhart and Livermore, *Global Youth Ministry*, under "Essential Questions for Global Youth Ministry," Kindle.

was in previous churches. It was time to reach out, stretch, and get involved."[12]

Years ago, while I was serving as a youth pastor in Florida, one of the relatives of one of our African-American youth passed away. In a show of support, I went to the funeral that was being held at an African-American church. When I arrived, I noticed that out of the three hundred or so guests, I was the only Anglo in attendance and I am ashamed to say I felt very much out of my comfort zone. However, the more we get out of our comfort zone, the easier it is to do. If we do it often enough, we discover that what was once uncomfortable, is now comfortable. I was surprised how true this was when I was recently teaching at a youth ministry weekend with our Filipino congregation. During dinner, the second night of the event, I looked around the dinner table at the twenty-five or so people and said in a suppressed voice, "I'm the only white person here!" The Filipinos laughed and said, "Pastor, are you only now noticing that?"

The reality is that Jesus never asked His followers to be comfortable. Quite the opposite in fact! Jesus told His disciples, "If anyone would come after me, he must deny himself and take up his cross and follow me (Matt. 16:24)." Just as Peter, Paul, and Phillip intentionally left their comfort zones to share the gospel cross-culturally, a healthy multicultural youth ministry must be intentional about leaving its comfort zone and interacting with people from other races and cultures.[13]

---

[12] Woo, The Color of Church, 114.

[13] Mark DeYmaz, *Building a Healthy Multi-Ethnic Church* (San Francisco, CA: John Wiley & Sons, Inc., 2007), under "Foreword," Kindle.

Culturally Diverse Leadership

In a healthy multicultural youth ministry, one will also find a culturally diverse leadership team. At Vienna Christian Center, there are over 25 cultures represented in the youth ministry, and the youth ministry leadership team is equally diverse, with leaders from Romania, Nigeria, Bulgaria, Austria, and Ghana, to name a few. Why are so many cultures represented? Because leadership and people's perception of leadership have their basis in a person's culture. Many people wrongly assume there is only one style of leadership or a "biblical style" of leadership. However, Plueddemann points out this error in *Leading across Cultures*:

> Megachurches often conduct leadership seminars around the world. Such seminars may make the naïve assumption that leadership is culture-free and that anyone from any cultures can teach it. They often claim they are teaching the "biblical model" of leadership, not realizing that the way they read the Bible is already influenced by their cultural theories about leadership.[14]

By having different cultures on the youth leadership team, prudent youth leaders have a tremendous resource that allows them to see beyond their own cultural bias and view things thorough the cultural lens of others. Caution must be exercised, however, for we do not want to critique our culture through the lens of another culture. Rather, we must critique our "culture through the lens of the kingdom of God. Indeed, what constitutes sin and morality must be determined by biblical standards and not the mores of a society."[15]

---

[14] Plueddemann, Leading across Cultures, 27.

[15] Benny C. Aker and Gary B. McGee, eds., *Signs and Wonders in Ministry Today* (Springfield, MO: Gospel Pub House, 1996), 65.

Additionally, minorities feel more included in churches when they feel they have a full partnership in leadership and worship structures of the church and are not just mere tokens. That is to say, when they observe people from their culture or ethnicity in partnership with the church leadership, and other key ministry structures of the church, they feel more accepted by the church.[16] This is not to say that a church or youth ministry should staff with minorities simply to attempt to draw minorities. As one African-American pastor told Mark DeYmaz as he was developing a multicultural team, "It is only when you allow us to share your pulpit, to serve with you on the elder board or alongside you in apportioning the money that we will be truly one with you in the church."[17] Those who lead in youth ministry must have a shared vision of reaching teens with the gospel in addition to having godly character and agreeing to the doctrines of the church. Since youth pastors and leaders are intentionally sought after, why not go beyond our comfort zone of culture and ethnicity and see who the Lord may be calling to help us reach all *ethnos*?

As previously mentioned, the leadership in the early church was ethnically and culturally diverse (Acts 13). When Peter, a leader in the Early Church and one of Christ's closest disciples, began to segregate himself from the Gentile believers, Paul rebuked him for his behavior (Gal. 2:11-14). In keeping with the biblical model, pastors, youth pastors, and church leaders should consider building relationships outside their ethnic, cultural, and socioeconomic circles for the purpose of finding people of like faith and passion to reach teenagers with the gospel.

---

[16] Brad Christerson, Korie L. Edwards, and Michael O. Emerson, *Against All Odds: The Struggle for Racial Integration in Religious Organizations* (New York: NYU Press, 2005), 159.

[17] DeYmaz, Healthy Multi-Ethnic Church, 74.

Interestingly, when Dr. Woo's church started its multiethnic push, it was with the youth ministry. During the transition time when the church was without a pastor, the church board attempted to be helpful and hired a youth pastor, so the new pastor would not have to do so upon his arrival. The Anglo youth pastor did not seem to have the same vision as Woo for multiethnic ministry and was soon let go. All the while there was a young African-American man named James serving in the church who did have the same calling and vision as Woo, and eventually James became the youth pastor at Wilcrest Baptist Church.[18] Woo's restructuring of his staff was difficult, but the youth ministry soon became the vanguard for outreaches that would mark the beginning of the church's journey into multicultural ministry.

Those striving to have a healthy multicultural youth group must be intentional about maintaining connections outside their comfort zone of ethnicity and culture. They must cultivate relationships with pastors, youth pastors, and religious organizations of different cultures to learn, and possibly recruit, team members to work with them in reaching youth. Those who are brought on the team must share the same biblical values and have a passion for reaching youth of all ethnicities and cultures. Above all, they must not simply be "workers" or "figureheads," but actual partners in ministry.

Awareness of Power Distance

A healthy multicultural youth ministry will also have an understanding of culture. While having a familiarity with cultural characteristics is important, when it comes to leadership, one characteristic can shed light on how people are led and expect to be led. That characteristic is power distance. It is a given that power is unequally distributed in cultures.

---

[18] Woo, *The Color of Church*, 101-103, Kindle.

Some cultures have high power distance where the people at the top make all the decisions and tell the people at the bottom what to do. Other cultures have low power distance where the leaders collaborate with those under them in the leadership process. "Power distance can therefore be defined as the extent to which the less powerful members of institutions and organizations within a country expect and accept that power is distributed unequally."[19] For the youth leader, this cultural dimension is crucial in understanding how youth from other cultures expect to be led, how they learn, and how they relate to those in authority, as well as how conflict is resolved.

Teenagers and youth leaders from high power distance cultures usually expect the leaders to make decisions with little or no input from those who are following. They may also expect to be told by the leaders what to do, when to do it, and how it is done (whatever "it" may be). On the other hand, teenagers and leaders who are from low power distance cultures may expect to be consulted or give their input in most (if not all) the decisions that are made regarding the youth ministry. In low power distance cultures, it is not uncommon for employees to interact with their bosses freely, to call their boss by the first name, and even to express disagreement.[20] This can lead to all types of interesting scenarios when parents from high power distance cultures (such as the Philippines, China, or Nigeria) immigrate to a low power distance culture (such as Austria, the U.K., or the U.S.A.) and their teenagers grow up living in that tension. Youth leaders in a multicultural context must constantly evaluate the cultural power distance of the youth they are reaching. In

---

[19] Geert Hofstede, Gert Jan Hofstede, and Michael Minkov, *Cultures and Organizations: Software of the Mind*, 3rd ed. (New York: McGraw-Hill Education, 2010),, under "Power Distance Defined", Kindle.

[20] Afsaneh Nahavandi, *The Art and Science of Leadership*, 7th ed. (Essex, UK: Pearson Education Limited, 2015), 168.

one youth ministry, there could be teenagers who call the youth pastor by his or her first name (as they do in Austria), and Filipino teenagers who always call the leader by their title and may execute the *pagmamano*[21] when meeting. Each group would have its own "default" expectations of how the leader will lead the group and how others in the group should show their respect and follow the leader.

One of the goals of a healthy youth ministry is to teach teenagers how to be disciples of Christ. Power distance also plays a part in how people learn, and understanding this cultural dimension will help provide an atmosphere conducive to this goal. In 2008, I was attending the University of Alcalá in Madrid, Spain. The majority of the other students in the class were young Chinese students who were in Spain to become proficient in *Castellano* Spanish. The teacher was a young Spaniard who was either ignorant of, or oblivious to, the fact that Chinese culture is very different from Spanish culture. This teacher would castigate the students for not asking questions and belittle them if they did not make eye contact with him. It is typical for Chinese students not to ask questions in a classroom. To do so would be disrespectful to the teacher and imply that the teacher had not adequately explained the subject matter. In the West, eye contact is considered a polite way of indicating a person is attentive to what is being said. In high power distance cultures such as China, eye contact is considered rude or challenging behavior, something a Chinese student would never think of doing in the classroom. This does not necessarily mean that Chinese teenagers will never ask a question or make eye contact in a multicultural youth group, but rather the youth leaders should have the awareness of *why* they may not be asking questions or making eye contact.

---

[21] The *pagmamano* is a sign of respect in Filipino culture, in which a person takes someone's hand and presses the hand to his or her own forehead.

As the pastors who transitioned from monolingual Latino churches to bilingual multicultural churches discovered, addressing issues patiently and lovingly can help ease transitions among cultures. Being in front of the teenagers or youth leaders and saying something like, "Because we have many different cultures here and we do not want to offend anyone and we want to follow the biblical mandate of honoring those in authority, we address our Pastors here as Pastor John, or Pastor Paul, etc.," can help defuse tensions and create unity.

Reflection Questions

- In what ways have you been intentional about reaching teenagers from different cultures and ethnicities?
- How do you encourage your leaders to get out of their comfort zone to reach people that are from different cultures and ethnicities?
- In what ways are you developing a leadership team that is multicultural / multiethnic?
- In what ways are you personally developing relationships across cultures and ethnicities?
- What is the power distance of your culture? What is the power distance of the group you are trying to reach? If there are significant differences, what will you do to manage the potential frustration level?

Now What?

- Schedule a strategic planning meeting with your pastors and church leaders. Based on your demographic research, determine the cultures and/or ethnic groups you will be intentional in reaching.

- List some changes you may need to make in your leadership structure to successfully reach these groups with the gospel.
- Once the church leadership is in agreement on how to proceed, cast your vision to the lay leadership and the youth ministry leaders.

Chapter 7

Language and Communication

It can be challenging to share the gospel if you cannot speak someone's language. This is why virtually all missionaries spend significant time in language acquisition. For many missionaries, this is one of the most challenging aspects of the missions call. To go from being a successful pastor or preacher, where they were able to fluently and eloquently communicate the gospel, to being someone who babbles like a five-year-old can be quite a blow to the ego. The tome, *Communicating Christ Cross-Culturally: An Introduction to Missionary Communication* by David Hesselgrave, contains over six hundred pages of insightful information for those who wish to communicate effectively across cultures. While there is much useful information on communicating cross culturally, and much of it would be applicable to multicultural youth ministry, it is beyond the scope of this work to reiterate the huge amount of material that has been written about cross-cultural communication. For this project, however, several themes of language and communication have seemed to appear repeatedly. These themes are an awareness of high-context verses low-context communication, awareness of fluency, and the awareness of body language.

Awareness of Context

A healthy multicultural youth ministry should have an awareness of context in communication. In his book, *The Silent Language*, anthropologist Edward T. Hall writes about high-context and low-context communication in cultures. People from high-context (HC) cultures tend to use body language, facial expressions, and voice inflection to help communicate the message. The content of the message is not specifically spelled out; rather, the listener assumes the context based on the HC messages the speaker is giving.[1] To those in HC cultures, "everything in the physical setting communicates something significant: the atmosphere in the room, the sounds, the smells, the expression on faces, the body language."[2] Additionally, HC cultures tend to place a high value on peace and harmony. The cooperation and the good of the group are more important than the individual.[3] Thus, HC cultures tend to avoid direct yes or no answers but rather answer in an indirect way that merely implies yes or no. Imagine the following scenario: A youth minister from a low-context culture asks a low-context question to a high-context teenager or youth leader. Not wanting to offend the minister by a direct answer in the negative, the HC listener may give a HC negative response that the low-context leader takes as affirmative. High-context cultures tend to come from South America, Asia, Africa, and the Middle East.[4]

Low-context (LC) communication, on the other hand, is the opposite of HC communication.[5] The majority of the information is explicitly within the written or spoken message, with little to guess. Figure 3 illustrates the difference between the two types of

---

[1] Edward T. Hall, *Beyond Culture* (New York: Anchor Books, 1989), 91.

[2] Plueddemann, Leading across Cultures, 78.

[3] Ibid., 79.

[4] Ibid., 78.

[5] Hall, Beyond Culture, 91.

communication. The lower the context, the more information is delivered, the higher the context, the less information is passed on, but the greater the context. Low-context communication is direct, with little ambiguity, and can generally be understood by people from both LC and HC cultures. Those leading a healthy multicultural youth ministry should have the awareness that tensions can rise by hidden messages within context that are not decoded. People from HC cultures can seem untruthful and perplexing to people from LC cultures while people from LC cultures can appear to be emotionless and indifferent to people from HC cultures.[6] Americans tend to be low context communicators; however, people from some parts of the world are even lower context communicators. These include Scandinavians, Germans, and German-speaking Swiss.[7]

Figure 3: High Context vs. Low Context Communication

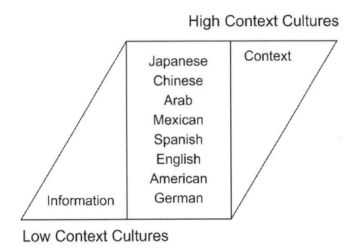

---

[6] Plueddemann, Leading across Cultures, 79.

[7] Hall, Beyond Culture, 91.

At a youth conference in Vienna, Austria, I wanted to illustrate some of the differences between HC communication and LC communication to a group of Americans and Austrians (both LC cultures). During lunch, I asked them to hang out with me in the kitchen and observe while we offered *Bergkäse*, or mountain cheese, to the conference guests. Now *Bergkäse* is a very strong-smelling cheese. Some have likened the odor of this particular cheese to an old garbage can that has been in the summer sun too long. When we offered the cheese to those from LC cultures, almost always they responded with a disgusted face and a very strong "No!" A young Filipino man (HC culture) took one whiff of the cheese and responded with a slight turn of the head and a mild look of disgust and responded, "Maybe not." Notice the difference in the responses? Both cultures responded strongly in the negative, but the HC communicator gave a "softer" response as not to offend the person offering the food. On a side note, *Bergkäse* is quite tasty after you get past the smell.

In a healthy multicultural youth ministry, prudent leaders will understand that some of the teenagers or parents may communicate in a context different from their own. The leaders will take steps to ensure that they communicate clearly and show the warmth and care that other cultures expect from their leaders in the way that they communicate. This does not necessarily mean that a LC communicator will need to become a HC communicator, but rather leaders will gain fluency in communication, so they have a situational awareness that they are communicating concern and warmth while being understood.

Awareness of Fluency

Webster sat on the back row of the church patiently waiting for me to join him as the last few stragglers left the sanctuary after the International Service had concluded. Webster was 15 years old and had recently emigrated from Zimbabwe to Austria. We had spoken several times before about his transition from Africa to Europe and some of the struggles that he had faced being in the German speaking public school system. Each time we spoke, Webster wore a look of frustration and anger on his face and I was having difficulty placing the source of those emotions. Prior to this meeting, however, I had met with Princess. Princess was a student at one of the local universities, was fluent in German and English and, as a Zimbabwean, fluent in Webster's native language. During my meeting with Princess, I asked her to fill in some of my gaps on Zimbabwean culture. Some of the information she shared with me about the education system in Zimbabwe began to connect the dots in my mind as a possible source of Webster's anger and frustration. As I approached Webster that Sunday morning, Princess was with me. I introduced them to each other and asked Webster if it would be alright if Princess translated for us. He gave his consent and Princess began to interpret for us. As soon as she began to translate, the look of anger and frustration that had been plaguing Webster's face disappeared. As I had suspected, the source of Webster's irritation was at his own lack of fluency in English! He had problems he wanted to talk over with his pastor, but he didn't know the words in English to adequately convey what he was feeling and experiencing. This critical understanding of fluency should be present in a healthy multicultural youth ministry. Whether it is counseling a student like Webster or the parents of a Latino teen who speak little English, we should be careful to assess the fluency of those we are ministering to in a multicultural context.

As more and more churches engage in multicultural ministry, sooner or later they will begin to minister to people who speak little or no English. This can be problematic as only 25 percent of American adults can converse in a second language.[8] However, this may not be an issue from teens who emigrate from Europe to other English-speaking

---

[8] Kat Devlin, "Learning a Foreign Language a 'Must' in Europe, Not So in America," Pew Research Center, July 13, 2015.

countries since the vast majority of teenagers (77 percent) in the European Union study English.[9] Nevertheless, having a working knowledge of a language and being fluent in the language can be two different things, and a discerning multicultural youth ministry will be aware of this issue. Think of all the expressions, colloquialism, and idioms that are used in everyday English, especially in youth ministry. What is a teenager, with limited fluency in English, to think when his or her youth pastors say things like, "Stop beating around the bush," or "Is there something you want to get off your chest?" or "Cat got your tongue?" While I was serving as a missionary in Spain, a Romanian friend named Pablo once asked in English, "Ashley [an American coworker] said I shouldn't be having a cow. Why can't I have a cow? Can I have two cows?" Although Pablo was fluent in English, Spanish, and Romanian, he was not fluent enough to understand that when Ashley said, "Don't have a cow!" she meant, "Don't get excited or upset."

Sometimes the issue with fluency is not due to a lack of understanding of the language, but rather the new language does not have the tools to completely convey the thought. One example is the Spanish word, *confianza*. Translated from Spanish, it can mean "trust"; however, the meaning in Spanish is much richer and deeper. It implies a deep mutual relationship in which a person is expected to give and receive special treatment. Dr. Judith Lingenfelter experienced something similar to this when she was teaching colors to her Head Start students on the island of Yap in Micronesia. The children were able to repeat the colors on a color wheel until she came to blue and green; at this point the students hesitated. On the small island in the Pacific Ocean, the Yapese have many words to describe all the variations of blue and green of the ocean, which is necessary in order for them to live in their

---

[9] Bridget Parker, "More Than Any Other Foreign Language, European Youths Learn English," Pew Research Center, October 8, 2015.

surroundings.[10] So the simple words, *blue* and *green,* did not quite convey what the children were actually seeing.

It can be frustrating for teenagers to try to express their feelings, emotions, and spiritual struggles to their pastors and church leaders when they do not have the words to do so. A friend of mine recounted how, after growing up as a missionary kid in Latin America and speaking Spanish all the time, he found himself in elementary school in the United States during furlough. One day in class, a boy began to bother him, but he could not remember the word for *bother* in English. So, my friend blurted out to the entire class, "Teacher, this boy is molesting me!" The teacher was probably shocked and horrified that he used the word *molesting.* However, *molestar* in Spanish means to "bother" or "annoy." A healthy multicultural youth ministry will not disparage or chastise youth for their lack of fluency, but rather they will be careful to ensure that the language the ministry uses is easily understandable for the teens. This may mean restating information in various ways, explaining idioms and expressions, and asking for clarity when they think there may be miscommunication.

Some churches have used language fluency as a tool to reach youth from other cultures within their communities. Justin Weaver was the youth pastor at Fortress Church in San Antonio, Texas. The church was a multi-congregational church with an English-speaking congregation (led by a Latino pastor) and a Latino congregation (also led by a Latino pastor). Many of the adults who attended the Latino congregation spoke little or no English, yet they had their teenagers attend the Fortress youth group that was conducted in English. Many of those Spanish-speaking parents wanted their children to go to the youth

---

[10] Lingenfelter and Lingenfelter, *Teaching Cross-Culturally,* 31.

61

group so they could learn English, increase their fluency, and better themselves.[11]

Awareness of Body Language

A third aspect of communication that leaders in a multicultural youth ministry should be cognizant of is body language. Body language can consist of gestures people use when communicating, physical contact (or the lack thereof), and personal space. If people in the United States stick their tongue out at other persons, usually it is a sign of contempt; however, in Tibet the same gesture is a friendly greeting.[12] Gestures that are commonly used in one culture may not necessarily be used in others; in fact, the same gesture could have an entirely different meaning and possibly be insulting. The "peace sign" and the "rock on" hand gesture (which resembles the "I Love You" symbol in American Sign Language) are commonly used by people in the United States. In many Latin American and Mediterranean countries, however, the "rock on" gesture is extremely offensive, and the "peace symbol" with palm inward is offensive in the United Kingdom and Ireland.

Body language used by other cultures can also be misconstrued by North American and European cultures. In Nigeria and Saudi Arabia, for example, it is perfectly normal for two heterosexual males to hold hands in public. Rather than being a sign of homosexuality, it is a sign of close friendship and camaraderie. In some Latin American cultures, people point with their lips rather than their fingers, and cultures such as Japanese and Filipinos keep their palm facing down when they call people to come, while the Hausa tribe of Nigeria and Americans keep

---

[11] Justin Weaver, interview by author, February 1, 2016.

[12] David J. Hesselgrave, Communicating Christ Cross-Culturally: An Introduction to Missionary Communication, 2nd ed. (Grand Rapids, MI: Zondervan, 1991), 420.

the palm facing up for the same gesture.[13] In some countries, such as Spain, it is very important to greet friends with the *beso*, or a kiss on both cheeks; equally important, when it is time to depart, the *beso* is given again.

Our cultural proclivities of body language are deeply ingrained in us. I was made keenly aware of this fact during one of our Celebration Services at Vienna Christian Center.[14] This particular Celebration service was being held outside on a warm summer day at a large park in Vienna. During the service, I greeted one of the Nigerian men I had been coaching in youth ministry. The gentleman stepped close to me (well within my "American" bubble of personal space) held my hand and spoke enthusiastically about the exciting changes he was seeing in the youth. Needless to say, I did not hear very much of what he was saying. Alarm bells were ringing in my mind as my culture was screaming at me, "There is man in your personal space! And he is holding your hand!!" One part of me wanted to shake his hand loose and take a step back, but another part of me knew that if I took that action, I would send a strong, non-verbal message that would damage the relationship. What would be more beneficial for the kingdom of God? Should I go back to my comfort zone and damage the relationship I had worked hard to cultivate or be uncomfortable and talk youth ministry? Honestly, it seemed like the longest ten minutes of my life standing in the middle of the park before God and everyone else, but it was well worth it as the relationship was solidified.

In a healthy multicultural youth ministry, there should be an awareness of appropriate body language. What is "appropriate" touch?

---

[13] Hesselgrave, Communicating Christ Cross-Culturally, 418.

[14] A Celebration Services is a special service that happens three times a year when all the congregations that make up Vienna Christian Center come together for a Celebratory worship service.

What is the correct amount of personal space? What are they saying to me with their body language? What am I saying to them with my body language? Youth leaders who are asking these types of questions will soon discover the answer, sometimes in humorous or slightly embarrassing ways. As they minister in a multicultural context, it will soon become second nature for them to find the "Goldilocks Zone"— not too close as to be inappropriate, and not too far as to seem relationally cold.

Reflection Questions

- Personally, are you a high context or low context communicator? What can you do to be better understood by people of a different context?

- If you are a Low Context communicator, what are some ways that you can say "no" to High Context communicators that will preserve the relationship?

- What are some idiomatic expressions that you use that someone from another culture may have difficulty understanding?

- What are some ways that you can communicate with teenagers or their parents who are not fluent in the indigenous language of the country in which you are serving?

Now What?

- Using the Internet, discover if the cultures represented in your ministry area are high context or low context.

- List some strategies that you will use to communicate clearly to all the cultures you are reaching.

- If language is a barrier, identify people in your church that have some fluency in the language that can help with communication.

- Outline how you can leverage technology to your advantage in communicating across cultures. Determine which of these ways would work best in your context.

Chapter 8

———— ∞ ————

Ministry Structures

Within the local church, there are structures that allow the church to function in such a way that ministry is relevant to the cultures they are reaching. Step into any rural church in the American Southeast, and you will typically find a different style of worship and different types of ministry than in the American Northeast or Northwest. Within the context of ministry structures in a healthy multicultural youth ministry, the leaders should have an awareness of time tensions, individuality, and worship styles.

Awareness of Time Tensions

Virtually everyone who has been involved in ministry has noticed some people tend to always arrive at church late. In some settings, this has caused a great deal of friction among people who are time conscious and feel that those who are late are being disrespectful to the Lord, the preacher, and the rest of God's people who are distracted when the latecomer arrives. On the other hand, these time-conscious people are often the first to complain if the sermon goes fifteen minutes over its allotted time. Broadly speaking, individuals and cultures tend to be Event-Oriented or Time-Oriented. Table 1: Time and Event Orientations illustrates some of the differences between these time orientations. Event-oriented cultures tend to be less concerned about when an event will start and end, and more concerned with what will happen at the event. This characteristic is often seen in the length of church services for some ethnic groups such as Hispanic and Korean, whose services rarely begin on time and often last two hours or more.[1]

Table 1: Time and Event Orientations

Time Oriented	Event Oriented
• Concern for punctuality and amount of time expended.	• Concern for details of the event, regardless of time required.
• Careful allocation of time to achieve the maximum within set limits.	• Exhaustive consideration of a problem until resolved.
• Tightly scheduled, goal-directed activities.	• A "let come what may" outlook not tied to any precise schedule.
• Rewards offered as incentives for efficient use of time.	• Stress on completing the event as a reward in itself.
• Emphasis on dates and history.	• Emphasis on present experience rather than the past or future.

Source: Sherwood G. Lingenfelter and Marvin K. Mayers, *Ministering Cross-Culturally: An Incarnational Model for Personal Relationships*, 2nd ed., © 2003 Baker Academic, a division of Baker Publishing Group. Used by permission.

---

[1] Sherwood G. Lingenfelter and Marvin K. Mayers, *Ministering Cross-Culturally: an Incarnational Model for Personal Relationships*, 2nd ed. (Grand Rapids, MI: Baker Academic, 2003), 42.

Time-oriented cultures such as German, Swiss, and American tend to be more concerned about punctuality and staying on schedule. "Each day is organized into time periods of specific length, and the use of each period is carefully planned."[2] People who are time-oriented usually have goals that they have set for themselves each day, and failure to meet these goals may make them feel as if they did not accomplish anything. As previously mentioned, a culture's time orientation is often seen in its worship service. When it starts and how long the services last are indicative of time or event-oriented cultures. Consider that in the United States the worship service for a predominantly Anglo congregation lasts 70 minutes while the worship service for an African-American church is 105 minutes. Anglos tend to be less event-oriented than African-Americans. In a multiethnic congregation, the worship service's average length is eighty-three minutes.[3] One of the tensions in multicultural youth ministry is finding the appropriate length of a youth service that meets the needs of all cultures involved.

A culture's orientation on time also determines how "late" is defined. Table 2: Concepts of Lateness demonstrates how "late" is defined with the North American, Latin American, and Yapese cultures. As can be seen, late is in the eye of the culture. Every week at Vienna Christian Center, the International Fellowship starts at 9:30 a.m., and every week people from many different event-oriented cultures arrive at 10:30 a.m. (or later) to enjoy the 120-minute-long service. After the service, the time-oriented people leave to continue their Sunday plans while the event-oriented people stay in the church café for up to an hour enjoying their coffee and spending time with their brothers and sisters in Christ. In the mind of event-oriented persons, they were not late; the time-oriented persons were early! In their mind, it is not about starting

---

[2] Ibid., 40.

[3] Yancey, *One Body, One Spirit*, under "Nonmusical Worship," Kindle.

on time, but rather about enjoying and making the most of spending time with the Lord in worship and with their brothers and sisters in Christ.

Table 2: Concepts of Lateness

	Lateness Excused	Tensions	Hostility
North American	5 minutes	15 minutes	30 minutes
Latin American	30 minutes	60 minutes	120 minutes
Yapese	120 minutes	180 minutes	240 minutes

Source: Sherwood G. Lingenfelter and Marvin K. Mayers, *Ministering Cross-Culturally: An Incarnational Model for Personal Relationships*, 2nd ed., © 2003 Baker Academic, a division of Baker Publishing Group. Used by permission.

This does not only effect the church service, but it will also impact meetings, when parents drop off, or pick up their teens from an events and special occasions. Let me give an example of how time-orientation can impact a special occasion. Our English speaking African congregation (AF) hosts perhaps half a dozen weddings per year. The weddings are elaborate, festive affairs with the wedding parties and many of the guests of African descent wearing traditional wedding garb. Often, the bride and groom will invite their Austrian friends and co-workers to the wedding. The invitation will state that the wedding will be at 11:00 and the Austrians (a time-oriented culture) will be there a few minutes before 11:00. When they arrive, they may wonder if the wedding has been called off. The church is decorated, the lights are on, but the only people there are other Austrian guests. It is not uncommon for African weddings to start an hour, or more, late. There have been occasions when the Lead Pastor (an American) would arrive "on time" to perform the wedding ceremony for the African congregation only to find no one at the church. One bride was over two hours "late" for her own wedding. This may be an extreme example, but it does illustrate that we should have a plan on how we are going to work with cultures with different time orientation.

It should also be noted that people from Time-Oriented cultures also tend to be monochronic, that is, they tend to focus on doing one thing at a time and concentrate on getting the task on hand done first before moving on to the next job. Event-Oriented cultures tend to be polychronic, that is, they tend to perform many tasks at the same time. It would not be uncommon for a leader from a polychronic culture to come "late" to a meeting and while at the meeting, send emails and take calls from others regarding things unrelated to the current meeting. This type of behavior could cause some consternation among monochronic colleagues, while at the same time the polychronic person has difficulty seeing why their monochronic associates put a task before people, especially when the ministry *is* people.

A healthy multicultural youth ministry will have evaluated if they are going to lean toward being more Time-Oriented or Event-Oriented. They will have determined what the appropriate length of the youth service and other youth activities will be and how they will handle the tensions that occur when people are "early or "late," as the case may be.

Awareness of Individualism

Most cultures in the world are collectivist. This is not used in the sense of a political system that controls people's lives, but rather it refers to the influence of the family or extended family over the individual.[4]

----

[4] Hofstede, Hofstede, and Minkov, *Cultures and Organizations*, under "The Individual and the Collective in Society", Kindle.

Missionary and anthropologist, Dr. Charles Kraft, clarifies the distinction between collectivist and individualistic cultures.

> Most societies seem to assume that it is good for persons and groups within that society to strongly value a cooperative relationship with each other. Working together would be seen as good and competing with each other as bad. In American society, however, we assume that competition between many individuals and groups in society is a good thing.[5]

Collectivist cultures tend to place more value on family and extended family relationships than individualistic cultures, and their loyalties are toward those structures. The following situation can help illustrate this point. You are in a building with your wife and mother. The building explodes into a fiery inferno, and you only have time to save one of the two women. Who do you save? Latin Americans, Southern Europeans and non-Westerners usually choose to save the mother. These collectivist cultures feel that, while you can replace a wife, you can never replace a mother. Northern Europeans and Americans tend to choose the wife, reflecting their individualistic culture.[6]

This awareness of individualism is important in multicultural youth ministry because it reflects the importance and hierarchy of relationships and impacts learning and discipleship. Many cultures that are Collectivistic in nature tend to learn better in group settings where there is little competition. Traditionally in these cultures, the older teach the younger, and when Westerners ignore this paradigm and attempt to befriend the student, respect is lost for the teacher and credibility is lost.[7]

---

[5] Charles H. Kraft, Christianity with Power: Your Worldview and Your Experience of the Supernatural, Reprint ed. (Eugene, OR: Wipf & Stock Pub, 2005), 186.

[6] Ibid., 189.

[7] Lingenfelter and Lingenfelter, Teaching Cross-Culturally, 42.

When discipling teenagers from such a culture, it may be sensible to disciple them in a group where they can work together on a Bible study lesson or group ministry project. In the West, it is generally held that if someone retakes a course, it is because he or she failed to master the material. In some Collectivistic cultures, it is not uncommon for students to repeat the same course to better understand. In the Philippines, for example, students would take a literacy training course three or four times before they felt ready to teach the course. The first time through the course, the students would familiarize themselves with the testing procedures, the teacher's style, and school context. The second time through the course, they would concentrate on the material and observe how the teacher taught; then the third time through would solidify the information, and the students would imitate the teacher.[8] Those students from highly individualistic cultures may fare better being discipled one on one. The key to this characteristic is understanding that teenagers from different cultures may respond better to different styles of teaching and discipleship.

This cultural dimension also influences how cultures view relationships. Accomplishing a task is more important in individualistic cultures than building relationships, but in collectivistic cultures tasks are accomplished through the development of relationships.[9] Filipinos score low (32) on the Hofstede scale of individualism (see Figure 2: The United States in Comparison with Austria and Philippines). This indicates they are a collectivistic culture and they value familial relationships. "For the Filipino, therefore, every social situation is an opportunity to acquire or enhance honor and to avoid incurring shame"[10] by "rightly" maintaining

---

[8] Ibid., 46.

[9] Plueddemann, Leading across Cultures, 120.

[10] Barbara E. Bowe, "Reading the Bible through Filipino Eyes," *Missiology: An International Review* 26, no. 3 (1998): 348

these relationships. When ministering to students from collectivistic cultures, it is important to also develop relationships with their family as well. While this is important to do for all youth, for collectivistic cultures, this seems to carry significantly more weight. To illustrate: When Youth Pastor Justin Weaver was serving at Fortress Church in San Antonio, where over 60 percent of the congregation was Latino, so many people from the congregation showed up at the hospital during the birth of his first child that nurses had to bring in extra chairs. When Justin's wife gave birth to their second child, they were serving at a mostly Anglo church, and only a handful of people visited them in the hospital.[11] While neither culture was right or wrong in the way they showed care and concern, this does serve to demonstrate the importance of family and extended family (even fictive kin) to collectivistic cultures. It also serves to illustrate how Justin was able to effectively cross into the Latino culture and effectively minister to the youth and their families.

Awareness of Worship

Perhaps no area in church ministry has been as controversial or contentious as worship. The old people in the church want to sing the songs from the hymnal or Dottie Rambo songs, while the middle-aged folks want to sing their favorite worship songs "off the wall," and it seems like the modern songs favored by teenagers repeat the same four lines over and over *ad nauseam*. George Barna reports that 25 percent of Protestant churches have experienced tension in the area of worship.[12] How much more complex is the issue when dealing with multiple

---

[11] Justin Weaver, interview by author, February 1, 2016.

[12] Barna Group, "Focus on 'Worship Wars' Hides the Real Issues Regarding Connection to God," *Articles in Faith and Christianity* (November 19, 2002): 1.

cultures! "When a church limits its style of worship to only one racial culture, it is sending out signals about who is supposed to be comfortable at its service."[13] Music is the language of a culture; that is to say each generation tends to have preferences in music different from their parents. In a multicultural church, steps are taken to help people worship God in ways that are relevant to them.

Mac Gervais is the minister of worship and youth pastor at Wilcrest Baptist Church in Houston, Texas. Wilcrest became a multicultural church under Dr. Rodney Woo and is well known for its cultural diversity. In the Sunday worship services, Mac leads worship using a mix of popular worship music in both English and Spanish that appeals to the Anglo and Latino cultures at Wilcrest. During their Wednesday youth services where there is a significant group of African-American students; Mac uses popular music from Hillsong as well as gospel fusion styles such as Israel Houghton.[14] Other multicultural youth ministries, such as the aforementioned *La Iglesia Alpha y Omega* in Miami, "incorporate rock and salsa music to communicate the gospel to English-dominate Hispanic youth."[15]

In addition to being mindful of musical worship differences, non-musical styles of worship have also been incorporated in healthy multicultural youth ministry. Filipino youth at Vienna Christian Center have dance teams that dance during worship services while Wilcrest Baptist youth ministry incorporates poetry nights and Spoken Word poetry made popular by artists such as Lecrae.[16] Some cultures (such as

---

[13] Yancey, *One Body, One Spirit*, under "Style," Kindle.

[14] Mac Gervais, interview with author, February 23, 2016.

[15] Rodriguez, "Hispanic Ministry," 196.

[16] Mac Gervais, interview with author, February 23, 2016. Examples of Spoken Word can be found on YouTube, such as "Lecrae –Tell the World."

Kenyan, Nigerian, and Latino) are very demonstrative in worship, coming to the front of the church and raising their hands or dancing to the music, while other cultures are reserved, preferring to quietly worship God. Other non-musical styles of worship could include the way the sermon is delivered, such as the "call and response" style of preaching found in many African-American churches, how the offering is received, and what genders can serve as ushers.[17] While it can be challenging, those involved in multicultural youth ministry explore different cultural worship and nonmusical worship styles and attempt to find ways of incorporating elements into the youth worship service.

Reflection Questions

- What is your personal time orientation? In what ways is this reflected in your ministry?
- What is the time orientation of the cultures within your community?
- How long is your typical youth service? Is it designed for Event-Oriented or Time-Oriented Cultures?
- What can you do to make your youth service friendlier to cultures with different time orientations?
- Does the worship in your youth ministry cater to one culture or ethnic group? What can you do to make the worship experience more inclusive to other cultures and ethnicities?
- What non-musical types of worship could you cultivate in your youth ministry that would appeal to a broad cross-section of the cultures you are trying to reach.

---

[17] Yancey, *One Body, One Spirit*, under "Non-Musical Worship," Kindle.

Now What?

- List some non-musical types of worship you could cultivate in your youth ministry that would appeal to a broad cross-section of the cultures you are trying to reach. Determine which ones you will begin to implement in your youth services and set a start date.

- List different musical styles of worship that would appeal to the cultures you are trying to reach. Work with your worship leaders to begin to implement these styles into your weekly worship.

- Examine the structure of your youth service. How much time is spent in worship? In fellowship? In ministry of the word and in prayer? Do any of these structures need to be adjusted to effectively minister to all the cultures you are reaching?

Chapter 9

◦◦

Final Thoughts

Although many churches in the world are monocultural, this was not God's plan from the beginning. Throughout the Old Testament, we see that God provided a way for people outside of Israel to come to know Him. In the New Testament, the paradigm shifted, and the people of God were to take the gospel to all *ethnos* across the world. The early church and its leadership were multicultural, but due to man's hard heart and disobedience to God, the Christian churches have become more homogenous and divided based on ethnicity and culture. Yet there is hope. More and more churches are recognizing that in Christ, "there is neither Jew nor Greek, slave nor free, male nor female, for you are all one in Christ Jesus" (Gal. 3:28). "When Christ abolished these distinctions, they did not cease to exist. Instead, they would no longer create barriers to fellowship with one another."[1]

While it seems that many of the churches in North American and Europe are still monocultural, a pronounced opportunity is facing the church. The current climate in immigration in both Europe and North America indicates continued growth of young immigrants arriving in these locations. The prevailing attitudes of teenagers indicate that they

---

[1] Rodney Woo, *The Color of Church* (Nashville, TN: B&H Publishing Group, 2009), 86, Kindle.

are open to crossing cultural and ethnic boundaries to develop friendships. Research seems to indicate that, more than pizza, there are commonalities in youth ministry worldwide, and among healthy multicultural youth ministries. While teenagers around the globe are perishing for not having heard the gospel, a healthy multicultural youth ministry that understands leadership, language, and communication and ministry structures could be an effective tool to introduce them to the love of God through Jesus Christ.

For youth leaders who are embracing the *Missio Dei* to reach youth of all *ethnos*, it appears as if the time is ripe to engage in multicultural youth ministry. By exhibiting cultural competency in Leadership, Language and Communication, and Ministry Structures, they can chart a course to establish a healthy multicultural youth ministry. While all teenagers could benefit from Affirmation, Acceptance, Appreciation, Affection, Availability, and Accountability within their local youth ministry, how affection or how acceptance is shown can vary from culture to culture. To effectively reach students from many cultures, it takes intentional leadership, and an understanding of communication and ministry structures. Admittedly, this is not easy. Youth ministry has never been "easy." It was not easy when Dave Wilkerson went to the streets of New York to reach teenagers like Nicky Cruz, and it is still not easy as youth pastors and leaders from across the world go to their "Jerusalem and Judea" to reach teenagers of all *ethnos* with the gospel. They go because they are called and because God has gifted them. Most of all, they go because they are led by the Holy Spirit just as Phillip was led to a desert road not quite sure what he would find. Indeed, with all its complexity and challenges, there is really no other way to build a healthy multicultural youth ministry than by being led *kata pneuma*, by the nudge of the Holy Spirit.

Index

Recommended Reading

DeYmaz, Mark. *Building a Healthy Multi-Ethnic Church*. San Francisco, CA: John Wiley & Sons, 2007.

Kageler, Len. "A Cross National Analysis of Church Based Youth Ministries." *The Journal of Youth Ministry* 8, no. 2 (2010): 49-69.

Lingenfelter, Judith E., and Sherwood G. Lingenfelter. Teaching Cross-Culturally: An Incarnation Model for Learning and Teaching. Grand Rapids, MI: Baker Academic, 2003.

Lingenfelter, Sherwood G., and Marvin K. Mayers. *Ministering Cross-Culturally: An Incarnational Model for Personal Relationships*. 2nd ed. Grand Rapids, MI: Baker Academic, 2003.

Linhart, Terry D., and David Livermore. *Global Youth Ministry: Reaching Adolescents around the World*. Ys Academic. New York, NY: Zondervan/Youth Specialties, 2011.

Ortiz, Manuel. One New People: Models for Developing a Multiethnic Church. Downers Grove, IL: IVP Academic, 1996.

Plueddemann, James E. Leading across Cultures: Effective Ministry and Mission in the Global Church. Downers Grove, IL: IVP Academic, 2009.

Woo, Rodney. *The Color of Church*. Nashville, TN: B&H Publishing Group, 2009.

Yancey, George. *One Body, One Spirit: Principles of Successful Multiracial Churches*. Downers Grove, IL: InterVarsity Press, 2003.

Bibliography

AG News. "A Vital Step Forward: The AG and UPCAG Unite." February 14, 2014. Accessed February 10, 2016. http://ag.org/top/News/index_articledetail.cfm?targetBay=c97d4d5c-a325-4921-9a9e-e9fbddd9cdce&Process=DisplayArticle&RSS _RSSContentID=27441 &RSS_OriginatingRSSFeedID=3359.

Aker, Benny C., and Gary B. McGee, eds. *Signs and Wonders in Ministry Today*. Springfield, MO: Gospel Publishing House, 1996.

Anderson, Monica. "African Immigrant Population in U.S. Steadily Climbs." Pew Research Center. November 2, 2015. Accessed December 1, 2015. http://pewrsr.ch/20o5CTT.

Ballard, Roger. "Race, Ethnicity and Culture." *New Directions in Sociology* (June 2002): 1-44. Accessed January 11, 2016. http://crossasia-repository.ub.uni-heidelberg.de/283/1/racecult.pdf.

Barclay, Thomas, to George Wood. January 16, 2010. Quoted in Scott Harrup. "A Larger Family." *The Pentecostal Evangel*, January 16, 2011. Accessed February 10, 2016. http://www.pe.ag.org/articles/index_2011.cfm?targetBay=ff479279-680e-4b02-ba0b-8f9ff830e632&ModID=2&Process=DisplayArticle &RSS_RSSContentID=18212&RSS_OriginatingChannelID=1321&RSS_OriginatingRSSFeedID=4677&RSS_Source=

Barna Group. "Focus on 'Worship Wars' Hides the Real Issues Regarding Connection to God." *Articles in Faith and Christianity* (November 19, 2002): 1. Accessed February 24, 2016. https://www.barna.org/component/content/article/5-barna-update/45-barna-update-sp-657/85-focus-on-qworship-warsq-hides-the-real-issues-regarding-connection-to-god#.Vs2iJJwrJhF.

Bowe, Barbara E. "Reading the Bible through Filipino Eyes." *Missiology: An International Review* 26, no. 3 (1998): 345-360.

Breckenridge, James, and Lillian Breckenridge. *What Color Is Your God? Multicultural Education in the Church.* Bridgepoint Books. Wheaton, IL: Baker Academic, 1995.

Brestak, Benjamin. Interview by author. Vienna, Austria. February 8, 2016.

Catholic Diocese of Arlington. "CDA Youth Ministry Manual--Multicultural Ministries." August, 2009. Accessed February 11, 2015. https://www.arlingtondiocese.org/youth/documents/ym-man_10-multiculturalministry.pdf.

Chappell, Paul. "Healing Movements." In *The Dictionary of Pentecostal and Charismatic Movements*, edited by Stanley Burgess and Gary McGee. Grand Rapids, MI: Zondervan, 1988.

Christerson, Brad, Korie L. Edwards, and Michael O. Emerson. *Against All Odds: The Struggle for Racial Integration in Religious Organizations.* New York: NYU Press, 2005.

Cohn, D'Vera. "Future Immigration Will Change the Face of America by 2065." Pew Research Center. October 5, 2015. Accessed February 10, 2016. http://pewrsr.ch/1Lbkz0o.

Connerley, Mary L., and Paul B. Pedersen. *Leadership in a Diverse and Multicultural Environment: Developing Awareness, Knowledge and Skill.* Thousand Oaks, CA: Sage Publications, 2005. Google Books.

Cooperative Fellowship Agreement between United Pentecostal Council of the Assemblies of God and Assemblies of God. February 14, 2014. Accessed February 10, 2016. http://ag.org/top/downloads/UPCAGCertif.pdf.

DeSliver, Drew. "Refugee Surge Brings Youth to an Aging Europe." Pew Research Center. October 8, 2015. Accessed December 1, 2015. http://pewrsr.ch/1LAHn06.

Devlin, Kat. "Learning a Foreign Language a 'Must' in Europe, Not So in America." Pew Research Center. July 13, 2015. Accessed February 23, 2016. http://pewrsr.ch/1L2FKai.

DeYmaz, Mark. *Building a Healthy Multi-Ethnic Church*. San Francisco, CA: John Wiley & Sons, 2007. Kindle.

Dougherty, Kevin D. "How Monochromatic Is Church Membership? Racial-Ethnic Diversity in Religious Community." *Sociology of Religion* 64, no. 1 (2003): 65-85.

Drury, Elizabeth. "Leading the Mutli-Ethnic Church: Help from New Metaphors and the Leadership Challenge." *Great Commission Research Journal* 2, no. 2 (Winter 2011): 225-26.

Emery-Wright, Steve. "Empowered to Worship: A Comparison of Youth Understandings of Worship between England and Singapore." *The Journal of Youth Ministry* 10, no. 1 (2011): 85-106. EBSCO.

Frizell, Sam. "Rachel Dolezal: I Was Born White." *Time*, November 2, 2015. Accessed January 20, 2016. http://time.com/4096959/rachel-dolezal-white/.

Garland, Diana R. *Family Ministry: A Comprehensive Guide*. 2nd ed. Downers Grove, IL: IVP Academic, 2012.

Gervais, Mac. Interview by Author. Vienna, Austria, February 23, 2016.

Hall, Edward T. *Beyond Culture*. New York: Anchor Books, 1989.

------. *The Hidden Dimension*. Garden City, NY: Anchor, 1990.

------. *The Silent Language.* New York: Anchor, 1973.

Harris, Ralph W., ed. *The Complete Biblical Library: New Testament Study Bible; Acts.* Chicago, IL: R.R. Donnelley and Sons Co., 1991.

Harrup, Scott. "A Larger Family." *The Pentecostal Evangel*, January 16, 2011. Accessed February 10, 2016. http://www.pe.ag.org/articles/index_2011.cfm?targetBay=ff479279-680e-4b02-ba0b-8f9ff830e632&ModID=2&Process=DisplayArticle&RSS_RSSContentID=18212&RSS_OriginatingChannelID=1321&RSS_OriginatingRSSFeedID=4677&RSS_Source=

Herrera, Linda. "What's New about Youth?" *Development & Change* 37, no. 6 (2006): 1425-1434. Accessed February 17, 2016. EBSCOhost.

Hesselgrave, David J. Communicating Christ Cross-Culturally: An Introduction to Missionary Communication. 2nd ed. Grand Rapids, MI: Zondervan, 1991.

Hiebert, Paul G. *Cultural Anthroplogy.* 2nd ed. New York: Baker Academic, 1997.

Hofstede, Geert. "Country Comparison." The Hofstede Center. Accessed January 19, 2016. http://geert-hofstede.com/countries.html.

------, Geert, Jan Hofstede, and Michael Minkov. *Cultures and Organizations: Software of the Mind.* 3rd ed. New York: McGraw-Hill Education, 2010. Kindle.

Kageler, Len. "A Cross National Analysis of Church Based Youth Ministries." *The Journal of Youth Ministry* 8, no. 2 (2010): 49-69.

Kraft, Charles H. Christianity with Power: Your Worldview and Your Experience of the Supernatural. Reprint ed. Eugene, OR: Wipf & Stock Pub, 2005.

Krogstad, Jens, and Mark Lopez. "Hispanic Population Reaches Record 55 Million, but Growth Has Cooled." Pew Research Center. June 25, 2015. Accessed December 1, 2015. http://pewrsr.ch/1TPuCQH.

------. "Puerto Ricans Leave in Record Numbers for Mainland U.S." Pew Research Center. October 14, 2015. Accessed December 1, 2015. http://pewrsr.ch/1PtcD0T.

Lingenfelter, Judith E., and Sherwood G. Lingenfelter. Teaching Cross-Culturally: An Incarnation Model for Learning and Teaching. Grand Rapids, MI: Baker Academic, 2003.

Lingenfelter, Sherwood G., and Marvin K. Mayers. *Ministering Cross-Culturally: An Incarnational Model for Personal Relationships.* 2nd ed. Grand Rapids, MI: Baker Academic, 2003.

Linhart, Terry D., and David Livermore. *Global Youth Ministry: Reaching Adolescents around the World.* Ys Academic. New York, NY: Zondervan/Youth Specialties, 2011. Kindle.

Livingston, J. Kevin. Missiology of the Road: Early Perspectives in David Bosch's Theology of Mission and Evangelism. Cambridge, UK: James Clarke & Co, 2014.

Lopez, Gustavo, and Eileen Patten. "The Impact of Slowing Immigration: Foreign-Born Share Falls Among 14 Largest U.S. Hispanic Origin Groups." Pew Research Center Hispanic Trends. September 15, 2015. Accessed February 10, 2016. http://pewrsr.ch/1J9RVLW.

Lucero, Arturo, and Robert Weaver. "Building Healthy Relationships in a Multi-Ethnic Congregation with No Ethnic Majority: A Case Study of Sunrise Church." *Great Commission Research Journal* 2, no. 2 (Winter 2011): 175-95.

Martin, Michelle, "Patrols to Block Expected 1.5 Million Refugees Flooding across Europe," *Sydney Morning Herald*, October 5, 2015. Accessed December 1, 2015. http://www.smh.com.au/

world/migrant-crisis/eu-and-turkey-have-struck-plan-to-stem-flow-of-
migrants-newspaper-20151004-gk140z.html.

Maxwell, John C. The 21 Irrefutable Laws of Leadership: Follow
Them and People Will Follow You. Rev. ed. Nashville, TN: Thomas
Nelson, 2007.

McDowell, Josh. The Disconnected Generation: Saving Our
Youth from Self-Destruction. Nashville: Thomas Nelson, 2000.

McGee, Gary. "William J. Seymour and the Azusa Street
Revival." Enrichment Journal (Fall 1999): 1-3. Accessed February 1,
2016. http://enrichmentjournal.ag.org/199904/index.cfm.

Metraux, A. "United Nations Economic and Security Council,
Statement by Experts on Problems of Race." American Anthropologist 53,
no. 1 (1951): 142-45.

Nahavandi, Afsaneh. The Art and Science of Leadership. 7th ed.
Essex, UK: Pearson Education Limited, 2015.

Nasr, Joseph, and Matthias Inverardi, "Anti-Migrant Protest
Turns Violent as German Welcome Cools," Reuters, January 9, 2016.
Accessed February 12, 2016. http://www.reuters.com/article/us-
germany-assaults-idUSKCN0UN0JQ20160109.

O'Neal, Sean S. Bridges to People. Maitland, FL: Xulon Press, 2007.

Ortiz, Manuel. One New People: Models for Developing a
Multiethnic Church. Downers Grove, IL: IVP Academic, 1996.

Parker, Bridget. "More Than Any Other Foreign Language,
European Youths Learn English." Pew Research Center. October 8,
2015. Accessed December 1, 2015. http://pewrsr.ch/1hsrlaG.

Penn State University. "In the Eye of the Beholder: A Global
Leader's Complex Reality." December 2, 2012. Accessed January 19,

2016. https://sites.psu.edu/leadership/2012/12/02/in-the-eye-of-the-beholder-a-global-leaders-complex-reality/.

Pew Research Center. "Almost All Millennials Accept Interracial Dating and Marriage." February 1, 2010. Accessed February 15, 2016. http://pewrsr.ch/UMEv1t.

------. "Modern Immigration Wave Brings 59 Million to U.S., Driving Population Growth and Change Through 2065: Views of Immigration's Impact on U.S. Society Mixed." Washington, D.C.: September 2015. Accessed January 10, 2016 http://www.pewhispanic.org/files/2015/09/2015-09-28_modern-immigration-wave_REPORT.pdf

Plueddemann, James E. Leading across Cultures: Effective Ministry and Mission in the Global Church. Downers Grove, IL: IVP Academic, 2009.

Quillian, Lincoln, and Mary E. Campbell. "Beyond Black and White: The Present and Future of Multiracial Friendship Segregation." *American Sociological Review* 68 (2003): 540-66.

Rodriguez, Daniel. "Hispanic Ministry Where Language Is No Barrier: Church Growth among U.S.-Born, English-Dominant Latinos." *Great Commission Research Journal* 1, no. 2 (2010): 189-201.

Southern Baptist Convention. "Resolution on Racial Reconciliation on the 150th Anniversary of the Southern Baptist Convention." Accessed February 1, 2016. http://www.sbc.net/resolutions/899/resolution-on-racial-reconciliation-on-the-150th-anniversary-of-the-southern-baptist-convention.

Vienna City Administration. *Vienna in Figures 2015*. Vienna, Austria: Vienna City Administration, 2015. Accessed February 17, 2016. https://www.wien.gv.at/statistik/pdf/viennainfigures.pdf.

Vine, W. E. *An Expository Dictionary of New Testament Words.* Nashville, TN: Thomas Nelson, 1985.

Waters, Mary. "Ethnic and Racial Identities of Second-Generation Black Immigrants in New York City." *International Migration Review* 28, no. 4 (1994): 795-820.

Weaver, Justin. Interview by Author. Vienna, Austria, February 1, 2016.

Whitesel, Robert. "The Five Types of Multicultural Churches." *Great Commission Research Journal* 6, no. 1 (Summer 2014): 22-35.

Woo, Rodney. *The Color of Church.* Nashville, TN: B&H Publishing Group, 2009. Kindle.

Yancey, George. *One Body, One Spirit: Principles of Successful Multiracial Churches.* Downers Grove, IL: InterVarsity Press, 2003. Kindle

.

Made in the USA
Columbia, SC
06 September 2021